Personal Finance

—Made Easy—

THE ESSENTIAL WORKBOOK TO
MANAGE YOUR MONEY WISELY

Alex A. Lluch

Author of Over 3 Million Books Sold!

WS Publishing Group
San Diego, California

3/09

Personal Finance Made Easy

By Alex A. Lluch

Published by WS Publishing Group
San Diego, CA 92119
Copyright © 2009 by WS Publishing Group

Designed by WS Publishing Group:
David Defenbaugh and Sarah Jang

$15.96

Photo Credits:
© moodboard/Corbis

For Inquiries:
Logon to www.WSPublishingGroup.com
E-mail: info@WSPublishingGroup.com

ISBN 13: 978-1-934386-32-3

Printed in China

INTRODUCTION 7

CHAPTER 1: YOUR FINANCIAL PICTURE 11
    Making Sense of Your Net Worth. 12
    Taking Action to Improve Your Financial Standing 13
    Several Ways to Increase the Money You Make. 14
    Your Expenses 16
    Are You in Financial Trouble? 16
    Average Living Expenses Worksheet 19
    Net Worth Worksheet 20

CHAPTER 2: ESTABLISHING YOUR GOALS 21
    Defining Your Financial Goals 21
    Paying Off Credit-Card Debt. 21
    Establishing an Emergency Reserve 21
    Saving Up for a Home Down Payment .22
    Saving for College 23
    Retirement Funds 23
    Establishing Goals Worksheet 25
    Needs and Wants Worksheet. 26

CHAPTER 3: BUDGETING AND SPENDING 27
    Constructing a Budget 27
    Common Spending Mistakes 28
        Impulsive Spending 28
        Spending "Imaginary Money" 29
        Spending with Credit Cards 29
        Spending Without Planning for the Future 29
        Emotional Spending 29
    Monthly Budget Worksheet 32
    Actual Monthly Expense Worksheet 36
    Year At a Glance: Savings Worksheet. 60
    Variable Expenses Annual Summary Worksheet 62
    Fixed Expenses Annual Summary Worksheet. 63
    Installment Expenses & Net Income Annual Summary Worksheets. 64
    Windfall Allocation Worksheet. 65
    Credit Card Purchase Worksheet 66
    Monthly Bill-Pay Worksheet 70

TABLE OF CONTENTS

CHAPTER 4: WAYS TO SAVE MONEY 75
    Utilities 75
    Food 77
    Fuel 78
    Clothing 79
    Entertainment 80
    Phone 82
    Car 82
    Rent 84
    Home Improvement and Maintenance 85

CHAPTER 5: UNDERSTANDING INTEREST RATES 87
    Interest Rates and Finance Charges in Plain English .87
    Mortgage Payment Calculator 88
    Payment Schedule for Fixed Rate Mortgage 90
    Interest and Savings Accounts 91
    Credit-Card Interest 92

CHAPTER 6: SAVINGS 93
    Banks 93
    Savings Account Options 93
    Certificate of Deposit 94
        Traditional 95
        Bump-Up CD 95
        Liquid CD 95
        Zero-Coupon CD 96
        Callable CD 96
        Brokered CD 96
        Money Market Account (MMA) 97
    Record of Savings Worksheet 99

CHAPTER 7: INVESTMENTS 101
    Stocks 101
    Bonds 103
    Mutual Funds 106
    Record of Investments Worksheet 110

CHAPTER 8: BUYING A HOME 111
    Renting Versus Owning 111

Good Reasons to Buy a Home. 114
The Use of Leverage 114
Bad Reasons to Buy a Home 114
Looking for a Home 115
Discount Real Estate Brokers 117
Common Sense Deals 117
Buy a Fixer-Upper. 117
Lowball Your Offer. 118
Evaluating the Asking Price 118
The Art of Making the Offer. 118
Dealing with the Counteroffer. 119
Securing a Loan. 120
Considerations for Singles 121
Considerations for Newlyweds 121
Considerations for Families 122
Considerations for Retirees 122
Being Approved for a Loan. 122
Appraisals and Inspections 123
Closing. 123

CHAPTER 9: RETIREMENT PLANNING 125
Individual Retirement Account (IRA). 125
Traditional IRA 126
Roth IRA 126
Social Security 128
Retirement Benefits 128
Survivor's Benefits 128
Social Security Disability Insurance Program. 129
Medicare. 129
Keogh Plans 130
401(k) Plans 131

CHAPTER 10: PERSONAL CREDIT 135
How Your Credit Score Is Determined. 135
The Consequences of Bad Credit 136
Fixing Your Credit. 137
Building Your Credit. 139

TABLE OF CONTENTS

CHAPTER 11: DEBT 141

    Good Debt, Bad Debt 141

    Eliminating Debt 142

    Managing Your Debt 143

    Credit Card Information Worksheet 145

    Debt Elimination Worksheet 146

    Determining Debt Payments Worksheet 148

CHAPTER 12: TAXES 149

    Beware of the Audit 152

    Income Tax Annual Summary Worksheet 154

    Tax-Deductible Expense Worksheet 155

    Your Paystub Explained 156

    Form W-2 Explained 157

    Form W-4 Explained 160

CHAPTER 13: INSURANCE 163

    Life Insurance 164

    Health/Dental Insurance 166

    Medicare 169

    Medicaid 170

    Disability Insurance 170

    Auto Insurance 172

    Homeowner's/Renters Insurance 174

    Home Inventory Worksheet 178

    Home Improvement Record Worksheet 180

CHAPTER 14: THE IMPORTANCE OF KEEPING RECORDS 181

    Documents Best Stored in a Safe Deposit Box 181

        Birth Certificates 181

        Death Certificates 181

        Passports and Citizenship Papers 181

        Divorce Decrees and Adoptions Papers 182

        Other Legal Documents 182

    Documents Best Stored at Home 182

CONCLUSION 183

INTRODUCTION

WHAT IS THIS BOOK ABOUT?

Personal Finance Made Easy unlocks the secrets of how people create and lose fortunes. Although the second is far easier than the first, becoming wealthy is more attainable than you've likely imagined—especially if you make just a few minor changes in the way you handle your financial affairs.

By reading this book, you will gain the financial knowledge, tools, and organizational skills you need to maximize your income, net worth, tax deductions, and savings. It also helps you make sound decisions regarding housing, day-to-day expenses, credit, and lifestyle. This important book helps you keep financial terminology straight, make smart investments, save money, and spend it wisely.

If you feel intimidated by the idea of taking control of your finances, you're not alone. Most of us prefer to focus on our jobs and leave financial management to experts. Many of us lack the necessary knowledge for handling our finances. Those who grew up in families that lived paycheck to paycheck often have no concept of what financial planning can do for them. Often we are overwhelmed by the hectic pace of life and simply lack the energy to handle our finances.

But taking a long, hard look at your finances is worth the time and effort. The following facts illustrate just how important it is to devote your time and attention to maximizing your wealth and earning power:

- Even though your children will probably be done with college and living on their own by the . . time you retire, your day-to-day expenses will be roughly the same as they are today.
- Social Security benefits will amount to just a fraction of your current salary.

Taking control of your finances and learning to make sound financial decisions is not as difficult as you might think. Those who look for ways to increase their income, watch their spending, and save regularly will end up financially secure.

WHO SHOULD READ THIS BOOK?

This book is for everyone who wants to save money, make wise financial decisions, and understand how to become wealthy. This book is for anyone who wants the choices and sense of control that wealth offers us. Researchers have discovered that the more control individuals have over their lives, the happier they are. Imagine having the money to retire early. You might well choose not to retire if you think that a day at the office is more engaging, exciting, and meaningful than a day on the tennis court. But wouldn't you prefer choosing to work rather than having to work?

It's never too late to begin making the sound financial decisions that will help you become wealthy. Indeed, wealth can be amassed at any time. Even those in their later years can benefit from taking charge of income and investment choices. Retirees are more likely to have the time to devote to finances. Without the competing demands of a full-time job, there's plenty of time to keep up on financial news, compare investment choices, and work with stockbrokers and bankers to make the most of income opportunities. In addition to being lucrative, it is also challenging and interesting to follow events in the world of finance.

While retirees can benefit from taking the time to understand and manipulate their assets and income, young people have the most to gain from getting their finances in order early in their life. Younger adults—that is, those in their twenties—face great financial challenges. If they attended college, they may well have student loans to repay; they often need to purchase a car; and they face paying for such necessities as insurance, housing, utilities, and food for the first time in their lives.

Even though they must pay for many things themselves, young people need to start saving as early as possible. Money that is carefully invested early has the greatest potential for growth. The more money that young adults can put aside for retirement and for a down payment on a home, the better off they'll be in the long run.

Many young people, if their parents have money, secretly count on inheriting the money they will need for their own retirement. This is a serious mistake. Your parents may have lots of money in the bank, and their mortgage may be paid off. But they're going to need money to pay for their health care. If they need to stay in a nursing home for very long, they may well have to sell their home just to cover their expenses. Just remember: the money they've saved is theirs, not yours.

Consider the following:

- The average baby boomer household has financial savings of less than $50,000, not counting the equity in their homes. The average savings increases to $110,000 if home equity is also included.
- Social Security will pay for only 30 to 40 percent of a household's expenses in retirement.

WHY YOU SHOULD READ THIS BOOK

We assume that you picked up this book because you would like to be wealthy. Your ambition may not be realized by next month or perhaps even in 10 years, but with shrewd planning, you could be wealthy in your later years.

For the purposes of this book, we'll consider "wealthy" to mean being in the top 10 percent of all income earners. In addition to income, most wealthy people share the following characteristics:

- They graduated from college
- They own their own home with a median value of over $350,000
- The majority of their financial assets (stocks/bonds) are handled by professional money managers
- They have no credit-card debt
- They have no auto loans
- They are often self-employed
- Their net worth (all assets minus all liabilities) is over $900,000

These characteristics must not be mistaken for an absolute formula for wealth. For instance, having no credit-card debt and no automobile loan does not mean that someone is rich; all it means is that most wealthy people are able to pay cash in full for their purchases and choose to do so.

The secret to accumulating wealth is living within your means—that is, spending less money than what you have coming in. Even wealthy people with very substantial incomes follow this rule. By living within their means, they never waste money by paying high interest rates on credit cards.

WHAT WILL THIS BOOK DO FOR YOU?

Reading this book will help you avoid some of the common financial mistakes that most people make.

Consider the following realities:

- On average, credit-card debt of Americans 65 to 69 years old has tripled in the last 10 years.
- As many as a quarter of all American families owe the maximum on their credit cards.
- More than 10 percent of American families are being hounded by collection agencies.
- Those within a mere 10 years of retirement commonly spend one-third of their income on debt payments.

The worst news is you are on your own when it comes to assuring your financial well-being. Structures of the past—such as Social Security—are no longer the pillars of financial well-being they once were. By the time you retire, there may be only one working adult paying taxes to support Social Security for every one person receiving benefits. Will there be enough money to support all of those who qualify for Social Security? Experts in Washington are trying to figure that out now. And as we've already noted, Social Security benefits will cover only 30 to 40 percent of your cost of living.

In the past, many people could count on receiving a pension from their former employer when they retired, but many companies no longer offer such benefits to their workers. Employers have turned away from pensions and toward 401(k)s and other savings programs that employees contribute to. What all this means is that you are your greatest asset in assuring your financial security. *Personal Finance Made Easy* will help you pave the way to your future and set you on the path to financial freedom and independence.

YOUR FINANCIAL PICTURE

Getting control of your finances begins with understanding your current financial situation. If you are feeling uncertain about your finances, your first move should be to take a good look at what you have (your assets) and how much you owe (your liabilities). Your total assets are equal to the cash you could raise if you sold everything you owned. Your liabilities consist of what you owe on such things as student loans, credit cards, and home and car loans. The difference between your assets and your liabilities is called your net worth. Knowing your net worth will make it possible to set your financial priorities.

If your net worth is greater than zero, that's encouraging news. If it's less than zero, don't panic. Having more liabilities than assets, known as negative net worth, is a fairly common situation. Most recent college graduates, for example, have a negative net worth. They may owe money for student loans, have borrowed money to buy a car, or have at least a small balance owed on a credit card or two. At the same time, most recent grads have no assets to speak of other than the clothes in their closet. Luckily, the liabilities of a recent college graduate are likely to be relatively modest. If they secure a well-paying job, there's an excellent chance they will be able to build up their assets even as they pay down their liabilities. They can, therefore, reasonably expect their negative net worth to turn positive at some point.

The key to building wealth is to understand your current financial picture. To do so, turn to the worksheet titled **Net Worth Worksheet**. Understanding just how much you are worth helps you decide:

· Where to invest
· What you need to save for retirement
· Whether you can afford to buy a home
· Whether you can start your own business
· Whether you can afford to have a baby
· Whether you can make expensive home improvements

Use your most recent bank statement to give you the balance in your checking or savings accounts. Do not count money that you might receive in the future. For example, don't include paychecks you expect to receive in coming months, and don't assume that the $100 you loaned your best friend will ever find its way back to your wallet. Some assets will be difficult to place a value on; be conservative in those cases. For example, the bicycle you paid $200 for 20 years ago is unlikely to be worth more than $25 today. Likewise, be cautious about listing as assets personal property such as jewelry or art collections. However, if you had an official appraisal done on such items, it's fair to use that figure.

Calculating your liabilities is likely to be considerably easier than estimating your assets. After all, your creditors keep close track of what you owe them. Chances are, you've got the most recent statements from the companies that issued your credit cards, student, car, or home loans. Somewhere on the statement a current balance will be shown. Add all of the current balances together.

Once you've totaled your assets and your liabilities, you're ready to calculate your net worth. Simply subtract your liabilities from your assets. Once you've taken this simple step, you've completed the easiest task. Now it's time to make sense of what you've learned.

MAKING SENSE OF YOUR NET WORTH

The following table approximates the average net worth of Americans in various age groups.

Table 1: Net Worth of the Average American According to Age

AGE	NET WORTH
Under 35	$20,000
35-44	$80,000
45-54	$150,000
55-64	$250,000
65-74	$200,000
75+	$160,000

As the table above indicates, Americans' net worth typically peaks just before retirement. Net worth begins to decline after age 64. This is probably due to retirees' drawing down their assets to meet their living expenses. They also may have begun "gifting" their wealth to heirs for tax and other reasons.

The relatively low average net worth for younger adults (those under 35) is hardly surprising. As we've already seen, those who are just finishing college and entering the work force often have at least some debt and relatively few assets. The important thing for younger adults to keep in mind is that if they track their net worth from one year to the next, they should see an increase.

If you are in your forties and feel that you are financially far ahead of other people your age (based on

Table 1), keep up the good work. If your net worth is lower than the average for your age group, this is the time to give some serious thought to your financial situation. You still have 20 to 30 years to create the financial cushion you'll need after you retire, but there's little time to waste.

Another way to judge your financial health is to compare your net worth to that of people with a similar level of education. Table 2 shows the average net worth for Americans grouped by how much schooling they've had.

Table 2: Approximate Net Worth According to Education Level

EDUCATION LEVEL	NET WORTH
No High School Diploma	$21,000
High School Diploma	$68,000
Some College	$69,000
College Degree	$230,000

These statistics will help you evaluate where you stand financially compared with others like you. If you are ahead, continue making sound financial decisions. If you are behind, it is time to start playing catch-up.

After calculating your net worth, you may be pleased or frightened. Those of you who are pleased with the amount you are saving still need to focus on building for the future. Those of you who are discouraged by how your situation compares to your peers should take heart. This is the first day of your new financial life. Now is the time to start building wealth so you can enjoy a comfortable life and even have enough money left over to pass along to your children.

TAKING ACTION TO IMPROVE YOUR FINANCIAL STANDING

There are few magic tricks to saving money and building wealth. Your net worth–indeed, your overall financial health–depends on one simple rule: spend less money than you bring in. Therefore, to increase your net worth you'll either have to increase your income, reduce your spending, or both.

Chances are you have less control over what you are paid than you do over your spending. But even if you only increase your income by $200 each month, in 25 years you will have earned an additional $60,000. Wisely invested, that extra cash could be worth far more than that.

SEVERAL WAYS TO INCREASE THE MONEY YOU MAKE

Start a small business

Lots of people find that they can turn a hobby or leisure activity into a part-time business. Consider what sorts of services you can provide in your spare time. If you're a do-it-yourselfer, for example, there's a good chance you can find someone who is willing to pay you to do simple repairs. If you're athletically inclined, your local school district may be willing to pay you to serve as a part-time coach or referee. Even people who simply like to run may find that busy pet owners will pay to have their dog exercised. The point is, the possibilities for side businesses are almost limitless.

Depending on where you live, opening a small business will require a certain amount of paperwork. For example, most local governments require anyone who operates a small business to obtain what is known as an assumed-name license—a document that serves as a public record of who actually owns a particular business.

In addition, your state may require you to obtain a sales-tax license so authorities can keep track of what you collect in sales tax. The federal government will also require you to obtain what is called a tax identification number so that the IRS can keep track of your tax payments. Finally, your local government may require you to obtain permits to operate your business. And if your business involves some sort of professional service, such as accounting or hair styling, there may be licensing requirements imposed by the state.

Of course, once you're ready to begin offering your services, you will want to let people know about your business. There are probably community newspapers that print small advertisements at very low cost. In addition, the Internet now makes it possible to reach thousands of potential customers through websites such as craigslist.com.

Get More Education

Many employers reward workers who continue their education or acquire new job skills. If you're working full-time, going to college to get a bachelor's or a graduate degree may be difficult, but the payoff in earning power is enormous. Community colleges offer dozens of courses designed for adults who are working full-time. In addition, most large universities have an extension division that caters to people who need a specialized course or two in order to qualify for a raise.

Ask For A Raise

Confronting the boss takes courage, but people often find that if they ask for a raise they get one. The secret to getting the raise you want is to have your arguments prepared when you knock on your manager's door. Knowing what other people with comparable jobs are being paid is a good start. The company you work for might be reluctant to publicize what your colleagues are being paid, but the Bureau of Labor Statistics (www.bls.gov/ncs/) lists current wage information for many fields. You can even search by both your job title and the state you live in. Use this information when negotiating your salary with your boss. Having these figures in hand will show him or her that you are serious and that you have done your homework.

You should be prepared to negotiate. Your boss is unlikely to respond to your first request by giving you everything you ask for, so be flexible. Even if you get turned down for a 10 percent raise, for example, you might be able to negotiate a raise of 5 percent now and another 5 percent a few months later.

Propose to Work Overtime

If you know that there is a project that keeps getting put on the back burner, you can propose to your boss that you take on the project after-hours. As with any business proposal, the more detailed you make your offer, the better. At the very least, you should be able to estimate with some assurance how much time the project will take and how much extra pay you want. If you can, demonstrate how the project will benefit your organization in terms of extra revenue or decreased long-term costs. That will increase your chances of getting the assignment.

Do a Promotional Push for Your Business

If you already own your own business, try to increase your revenue by advertising more broadly than you have done in the past. Attend conventions where you can display your wares or services to others in related businesses. If you're starting a new product line or a new service, throw a launch celebration. Or, an anniversary party for an older, established business can generate publicity. Be certain to invite members of the local media; community newspapers and local radio and television stations often look for such stories. Sponsor community events like concerts or fundraisers; anything that raises awareness of your name or your business's name can increase revenue.

Raise Your Fees

It is difficult to raise fees, but at times it is necessary and appropriate. Some business people worry that raising prices will drive customers away, but experts say that raising rates by 5 percent or less will not do that. Most customers will accept a small increase in fees rather than endure the headache of shopping their business around. Start by sending out a letter explaining the need for the increase. The tone in your letter should be matter-of-fact and friendly, not apologetic. Tell customers how long it's been since you last raised your rates; if it's been several years, they'll be more accepting of the increase. Provide some general idea of why you are raising rates—increased labor costs, fuel, supplies, and so on. There's no need to go into detail about how much profit you need or want for your business, but making it clear that you're not being arbitrary or greedy will make customers more open to the change. Close by saying that you have appreciated their business over the years and look forward to working with them in the future. There are many models for such business letters available on the Internet.

YOUR EXPENSES

How much you are paid may not be something that you can control, but data collected by the federal government makes one thing very clear: As our income increases, so does our spending. For example, people with annual incomes of around $150,000 spend about four times as much on clothing each month as people who make $35,000. Interestingly, the government's statistics show that as their income rises, people still spend about the same percentage of their income in categories such as food, housing, and transportation. This suggests that people buy what they think they can afford rather than what they need.

And yet, your spending is something you can control. For most of us, the hard part of controlling expenses is getting a clear idea of what those expenses are. The first step toward controlling expenses is to write down exactly what you spend your money on. The **Actual Monthly Expense Worksheet** in Chapter 3 lists the categories in which most people spend money. Fill in the obvious ones, such as rent, food, and insurance; if you have expenses that don't seem to fit into any category, there are blank spaces to create your own. (For example, if you are a teacher, you can create your own category for teaching materials.) Before you fill it out, make extra copies of this worksheet. That way, you can track your spending over several months.

One thing that makes controlling spending difficult is keeping track of minor purchases, such as meals at fast food restaurants or small items at convenience stores. Particularly if you pay cash, it's easy to forget that you've bought something at all. The best way to keep track of cash transactions is to save receipts. If the receipt isn't detailed, take a moment to write down what was purchased. Once you get home, stick the receipt on a spindle or put it in an envelope with receipts for other purchases. At the end of the month you can sort these receipts into the various categories you've identified, add up the totals, and record the amounts.

When you've finished adding up all your expenses, you may be surprised at how much you spend in some categories. As you look for ways to cut your expenses, focus on what is known as discretionary spending—purchases for items that you want but can get along without. Probably, you have no immediate hope of cutting your housing expenses unless you just happen to be on the verge of moving and know where to rent a much cheaper apartment or buy a less expensive house. Health care is something that you would be advised not to scrimp on. Scan your worksheet, though. Are there entertainment expenses that you could eliminate? Perhaps you can cut down on the number of restaurant meals. Or you could shift from golf (which can involve substantial costs for greens fees) to cycling or running as a way of getting your exercise. Chapter 4 will go into more detail on how you can cut down on spending.

ARE YOU IN FINANCIAL TROUBLE?

The answer to this question is, "It depends." If you're in your 20s and have just a few hundred dollars in the bank, and a monthly car payment to make, but find that you have $50 left over each month after the bills are paid, you're not in trouble. On the other hand, if you're 45 or 50 and in the same shape financially, that's not a good spot to be in; you've got some work to do.

Experts have identified a few milestones that we can all watch for as we track our financial progress. If you are in your 20s, you should strive to pay off any college loans and credit-card balances. This is the time you should be setting up the accounts that will eventually pay for your house or retirement. If you take these steps now, by your late-20s or early 30s there's a good chance that you will have enough saved up for a down payment on a home.

Those in their 30s should begin to see their net worth growing substantially. People in their 30s may have substantial debt in the form of a mortgage, but that's perfectly acceptable, since part of each month's payment is building equity in the home. Ideally, though, at 30-something you should have enough money left over at the end of every month to put into investments that will grow in value. This is the time for you to put as much money as you can into savings; if you have children, there will be college educations to pay for, probably within 20 years. (It's a mistake to hope that your children will put themselves through college, even if you managed to do so. Finance officials at both state and private colleges say that, on average, about 30 percent of students' tuition is paid by their parents.)

By the time they reach their 40s, most people should be well on their way to saving for retirement, even though they will probably be helping pay for their children's college education. At this point, they should have at least 30 or 40 percent of their mortgage paid off. If they have additional loans, they should be for home improvements that add substantially to the value of the house. Borrowing money to remodel the kitchen, for example, might well make sense, but borrowing to buy new furniture probably is not a good idea.

If you're in your 50s, your children's college educations should be paid for and you should have substantial retirement funds. Your home should be mostly paid for, and you should be otherwise debt-free.

People in their 60s and 70s who have planned well can rest easy. Usually mortgage payments are behind them. Entertainment expenses rise for people in this age category. That's actually desirable, since researchers say that retirees stay healthy longer if they stay busy.

No matter which decade of life you are in or how your situation compares to others your age, it is never too late to build your net worth. There are practical, easy-to-implement steps that will help you enhance your sense of financial well-being.

WORKSHEETS IN THIS CHAPTER:

· **Average Living Expenses Worksheet**: Use records such as receipts, your check-book register, credit card statements, etc., to write down what your family usually spends each month for food, housing and the other categories listed. Finally, figure out the percentage of take-home pay you spend for each category. To do this, divide the amount in each category by the total amount of take-home pay and multiply by 100.

For example, consider a family with a take-home pay of $3,000 per month. This family spent $600 for food (at home and away), so the percentage spent for food is 20 percent. ($600 divided by $3,000 = .20 x 100 = 20%)

Then, compare your percentages in each category to those in the pie chart showing the average American's expenses to see how you stack up against the nation's spending habits.

· **Net Worth Worksheet**: Use this worksheet to create an accurate picture of your net worth. Tally your assets and liabilities, and subtract liabilities from assets to calculate your net worth. Understanding your net worth, and recalculating it each year, is an important step in tracking your progress toward your financial goals and planning your estate.

TYPICAL EXPENSES ACCORDING TO INCOME

This pie chart shows the average American's spending habits for a calendar year. These figures are based on the Tax Foundation's (www.TaxFoundation.org) calculations for the chart titled: *How Many Days Per Year America Works to Pay Taxes Compared to Other Major Spending Categories.*

Note that there is no slice for Savings, as our savings rate is negative according to their calculations.

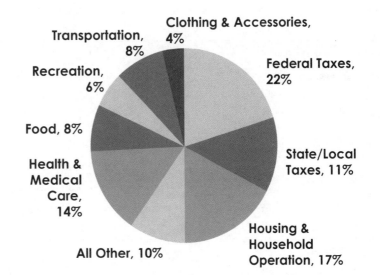

Average Living Expenses

Monthly Take-Home Pay = $			
Category	Average Monthly Expense	Percentage of Take-Home Pay	Percentage of Average American Take-Home Pay
Federal Taxes	$	%	22%
State/Local Taxes	$	%	11%
Housing & Household Operation	$	%	17%
Clothing & Accessories	$	%	4%
Transportation	$	%	8%
Recreation	$	%	6%
Food	$	%	8%
Health & Medical Care	$	%	14%
All Other	$	%	10%

NET WORTH WORKSHEET

Assets

Cash & Accounts

Cash	$
Checking	$
Savings	$
Money Market	$
Other:	$

Investments (current market value)

Life insurance cash value	$
Certificates of deposit	$
Savings bonds	$
Stocks	$
Bonds	$
Mutual funds	$
Annuities	$
IRA (Regular/Roth/Keogh plan)	$
401(k), 403(b), or 457 plans	$
Notes and loans receivable	$
Other:	$
Other:	$

Real Estate/Property (current market value)

Primary residence	$
Secondary residence	$
Land	$
Income property	$
Other:	$

Personal Property (current market value)

Automobiles	$
Recreation vehicles/watercraft	$
Jewelry	$
Collectibles and antiques	$
Electronics	$
Furnishings	$
Tools/Equipment	$
Other	$

Total Assets	$

Liabilities

Current Debts

Credit Card 1	$
Credit Card 2	$
Credit Card 3	$
Household	$
Medical	$
Legal	$
Alimony	$
Child support	$
Other:	$
Other:	$

Mortgages

Primary residence	$
Secondary residence	$
Land	$
Income property	$
Other:	$
Other:	$

Loans

Home equity	$
Bank/Finance Company 1	$
Bank/Finance Company 2	$
Automobile	$
Recreation vehicles/watercraft	$
Student	$
Personal loan	$
Retirement Accounts	$
Other:	$
Other:	$

Taxes

Back taxes	$
Other:	$
Other:	$
Other:	$

Total Liabilities	$

Total Assets		Total Liabilities		Net Worth
$	-	$	=	$

ESTABLISHING YOUR GOALS

Now that you have a better idea of what your financial situation is, you can begin setting some goals for yourself. Chances are, you already have some goals in place. For example, do you want to save up to go on a cruise someday? That's certainly a reasonable goal. Keeping that goal in mind will help you focus your efforts and save your money.

DEFINING YOUR FINANCIAL GOALS

To get your finances on track, you must define your goals clearly. Goals have to be time-sensitive. That is, you should impose a deadline of some sort. No matter what your age or financial situation, ask yourself what you want to accomplish with regard to your finances in a year, five years, or longer.

PAY OFF CREDIT-CARD DEBT

Financial professionals agree that eliminating credit-card debt is the very first step toward financial stability. Credit cards are one of the worst ways to be indebted because their issuers charge extremely high interest on unpaid balances. If you have a credit card, you may well have been promised a low introductory interest rate. Credit-card issuers commonly offer "teaser" rates of 7, 6, or even 0 percent, but those rates usually go up after a few months. As a result, you may well be paying the standard rate, which runs anywhere from 13 to 20 percent. On a $5,000 balance at a 15 percent rate, you will pay more than $750 per year in interest and finance charges. Additional charges, such as fees for any late payments, raise that figure even higher..

Because they cost you so much money in interest, paying off credit-card debt is one of the best moves you can make. The hundreds of dollars you save in interest charges can be put into any number of savings or investment accounts and make money for you, instead of the credit-card company.

ESTABLISHING AN EMERGENCY RESERVE

Once you've paid off any credit-card debt, the next step is to ensure that you stay out of debt. At least for the short term, you should try to build up a cash reserve equal to three to six months' living expenses. Such a reserve will allow you to pay your day-to-day expenses without having to charge purchases on your credit card in the event of an emergency. The need for such a reserve is not to be taken lightly. A seemingly secure job is anything but assured. Companies have been known to downsize, move their offices, and even go out of business. In addition, unforeseen medical emergencies or natural disasters can be very costly. No matter what the reason, if you lose your job you're probably going to have to survive for at least a short time without a paycheck. You will find it easier to search for a new job if you aren't worrying about how you're going to pay your rent or mortgage in the immediate future.

When you set up your emergency fund, be certain that it's in an account that you can draw money from easily. You won't want to have to wait for the funds to be available if you've got rent or a mortgage payment due. The account you establish should also not impose fees for pulling funds out of it. As you would when establishing any financial account, you should shop for the highest interest rate. If you really want to maximize the interest your money earns, you could invest in a three- or six-month Certificate of Deposit. Certificates of Deposit, or CDs, typically offer higher rates of return than traditional savings accounts do. For example, a traditional savings account may pay annual interest of less than one percent, while a CD may pay interest of 5 percent or more annually. CDs are easily cashed in, so you have ready access to your money. The only problem with a CD is that you may be charged an early-withdrawal fee if you cash it in before it matures. (Certificates of Deposit and other savings accounts will be discussed in further detail in Chapter 6.)

SAVING UP FOR A HOME DOWN PAYMENT

Millions of Americans see purchasing a home as the best way to build wealth. There's a good reason for people to feel this way. Because a portion of each monthly mortgage payment goes toward paying off the loan, buying a home increases your net worth by reducing debt and building your assets. In a very real sense, a home of your own is money in the bank. Better yet, over the long-term (five to seven years or more) home values usually increase—sometimes they double or even triple their purchase price in that time frame.

Therefore, after paying off credit-card debt and establishing an emergency savings account, buying a home is the next priority in assuring your long-term financial security. Experts caution that a home purchase should be considered a long-term investment, not a route to quick riches. Although homes in much of the U.S. soared in value during the late 1990s and the first years of the 21st century, such booms are unusual. If you buy a house, therefore, be prepared to stay in it for five or more years. That way, even if prices drop after you buy, you have a good chance of coming out ahead.

Another advantage to buying a home is that doing so helps protect you from inflation. As prices for goods and services rise (a condition known as inflation), rent goes up as well. But if you have what is known as a fixed mortgage, your house payment will not go up. We will further discuss the best ways to go about acquiring a mortgage and finding a home in Chapter 8.

Here's the bottom line: When setting your financial priorities, first pay off that high-interest debt. Then create an emergency account with a decent interest rate. Finally, buy a house. If you still have extra income, don't feel like you are in the money. You will need money to retire on, so begin a savings plan before you start putting money into your children's college savings account.

SAVING FOR COLLEGE

It's no secret that the largest expense that millions of Americans in their 40s or 50s face is paying for their children's college education. The tuition at four-year colleges and universities varies widely, but even at the least expensive institutions, the yearly cost of attending college (tuition, room and board, and miscellaneous fees) is likely to be more than $10,000. If a child chooses to attend a private college or go out-of-state, the cost increases enormously. Typically, a state-supported university charges 3 times as much tuition for an out-of-state student as it does for an in-state student. The tuition charged by private universities is on a par with out-of-state costs at public universities. On top of all the tuition and housing expenses, you will have to pay for textbooks, which can add hundreds of dollars to each year's expenses. What this all means is that if you have children, you need to start saving *now* if you expect to be much help in paying for their college education.

RETIREMENT FUNDS

As you set your goal for building your retirement nest egg, keep in mind that you cannot expect your living expenses to be significantly lower than they are now. Think about what you're spending money on today. Now ask yourself if you're planning to eat only twice a day instead of three times. Are you planning to run your furnace or air conditioner less just because you're retired? You'll still want to go to movies, eat out occasionally, and take vacations. In other words, most of what you spend money on today will not magically disappear. In addition, although your children will be grown up and on their own (you *hope*), as you age, you'll have other expenses you don't have now. Visits to doctors, medications, and other health care expenses will rise and will be only partially covered by various insurance payments.

We'll be discussing retirement planning in greater detail in Chapter 9. For now, though, just remember that your goals must include saving adequately for your retirement.

WORKSHEETS IN THIS CHAPTER:

- **Establishing Goals Worksheet**: Use this worksheet to write down, prioritize, and detail your short-range, mid-range, and long-range financial goals. Short-range goals are goals to be reached within the next year, such as taking a family vacation. Achieving these goals will give you motivation and confidence to reach your larger goals. Mid-range goals are those that should be accomplished within the next five years; for instance, buying a new car. Long-range goals are those beyond five years, including placing savings in a college account for your children. This worksheet will help you determine how much savings you will need to reach each of these milestones.

- **Needs and Wants Worksheet**: Purchases you make when you have extra discretionary money fall into two categories: needs (higher priority) and wants (lower priority). Needs and wants are different than goals in that they are more immediate and don't require long-term planning and accumulation of funds. This worksheet will help you prioritize your expenses into needs and wants to determine what you will buy when your improved financial planning allows you to have a leftover income. As you read this book, you will find you have more and more discretionary income available for your needs and wants.

Short-range Goals:

Priority	Description	Estimated date	Estimated cost	How to achieve this goal?

Mid-range Goals:

Priority	Description	Estimated date	Estimated cost	How to achieve this goal?

Long-range Goals:

Priority	Description	Estimated date	Estimated cost	How to achieve this goal?

NEEDS AND WANTS WORKSHEET

Needs:

Priority	Description	Date	Cost	How and where to obtain this item?

Wants:

Priority	Description	Date	Cost	How and where to obtain this item?

BUDGETING AND SPENDING

If you find that you have trouble living within your means—that is, you spend more money than you have coming in—you're not alone. And in a way, that shouldn't be too surprising. Children are rarely taught how to manage money. Most high schools require youngsters to take years of math and science, but the basics of money management get far less attention. As a result, many adults try to economize but have no idea where to begin.

Few will disagree with the idea that it is easier to spend money than earn it. Spending money is a part of life. You become a consumer when you purchase groceries, fill your gas tank, and buy a pack of gum. You spend money on your rent or mortgage, car insurance, and utilities. Spending money is something that is impossible to avoid, especially on the things we need in order to live.

CONSTRUCTING A BUDGET

Compile your receipts, paychecks, and account statements to determine how much money you've got coming in and where you're spending it. You can use these figures as you fill out the **Monthly Budget Worksheet** found at the end of this chapter. (It's a good idea to make several copies of the **Monthly Budget Worksheet** so that you can redo it in the future.)

As a first step in constructing a budget, examine your expenditures. What purchases or expenses were unavoidable? Rent, mortgage payments, or utilities would be examples of these necessities. Car payments are probably necessary—unless you're prepared to take public transit. Fuel for the car would count among your necessities as well. Clothes you wear regularly for work would also count as necessities. And if you've got a balance you owe on your credit card, don't forget to list a reasonable amount that you can afford to kick in to reduce that debt. Finally, follow a rule that virtually every finance expert advises: pay yourself first. That means setting aside an amount—no matter how small—to deposit in some kind of savings account before you begin spending what remains of your budget. Add up all the expenditures that seem necessary. That figure ought to be smaller than the amount of money you've got coming in.

Now, give yourself a pat on the back: You've just constructed a budget! Your task from now on is to avoid spending more than the amounts you've entered for each spending category. Budgets, though, are not meant to be carved in stone and should be subject to revision. For example, if fuel prices rise, you must adjust your budget for gasoline or diesel fuel accordingly. It's normal, therefore, to revise your budgeting worksheet over time.

Subtract your total necessary expenses from the amount of money you have coming in every month; the remainder constitutes disposable income—money that you can use in whatever way you wish. Of course, you can always funnel extra cash into your savings (even though some contribution to savings is already listed among your necessary expenses). But as long as you are saving something, the extra money can be used to pay for entertainment, hobbies, clothes shopping, and similar optional purchases.

Now add up all of your spending and subtract that figure from your income. If you're bringing in more money than you're spending and saving, that's great. The extra can be set aside to pay for a larger optional purchase, such as a luxury vacation or any number of items that make for a more comfortable lifestyle.

On the other hand, if you find that your income is just barely covering expenses and modest contributions to savings, you probably should look at ways to rein in discretionary spending. Take a moment and think about why you bought the things you didn't absolutely need. Perhaps you made some of your purchases on impulse—in such cases, you may not even be able to say why you bought certain items. Sometimes, too, we fall victim to peer pressure and join friends in going to a trendy new club or restaurant, even though we know we can't really afford to do so.

One problem with spending money is that it is easy to lose sight of how quickly small purchases can add up. We usually have little difficulty keeping track of large expenses like rent or car payments. But smaller, day-to-day purchases often wind up costing a far greater amount than most people realize. It is easy to forget that purchasing a $3 cup of coffee every day adds up to $90 at the end of the month. That adds up to more than $1,000 a year!

COMMON SPENDING MISTAKES

The good news is that we can control much of our spending. All it takes to cut our spending is to understand the kinds of mistakes people make and then avoid repeating those errors.

Impulsive Spending

Sometimes people make even a major purchase without first stopping to determine how they're going to pay for it. Such impulsive buying, when done with a credit card, can result in debt that can take years to pay off. If you purchase an expensive item for cash, you still need to keep in mind the impact on meeting your financial obligations. Will you have enough money to pay your rent or mortgage this month? Or will you have to put off paying down an existing balance on your credit card? Impulse buying, then, can quickly dig you into a very deep financial hole.

To avoid impulse purchases of the sort that can get you in trouble, always ask yourself if you really need the item in question. Almost always, the answer will be "no." But if you really do need the item you're looking at, try asking a couple of other questions: Will a less expensive model do the job? Can you buy the item at another store for a lower price? At the very least, asking questions like these will make your purchase less impulsive.

Spending "Imaginary Money"

If you're in your 20s or 30s, it's likely that birthdays, holidays, and other occasions bring you gifts in the form of cash. Likewise, depending on your job, you may reasonably expect an end-of-the-year bonus. Such windfalls allow you to buy items you otherwise might not be able to afford. Trouble can start, though, if you start spending money before you actually *receive* it. If your employer unexpectedly announces, for example, that business is down and there will be no profit-sharing bonuses, you can be stuck with a purchase you can no longer afford.

Spending with Credit Cards

Not only can credit cards allow you to buy items you don't need, they can cause you to pay more for items than is necessary. If you don't pay off your balance each month, you'll be charged up to 20 percent annual interest on the unpaid balance. That means purchases end up costing you far more than the amount shown on the price tag. Always remember that credit cards do not represent "free money." Just because you have access to a line of credit does not mean it is always appropriate to use it. Chapter 5, Understanding Interest Rates, discusses credit card interest rates in more depth.

Spending Without Planning for the Future

Another common mistake involves reckless spending in the present without regard for our future needs. Even if a purchase doesn't result in added debt, it takes money that could have been put aside for a down payment, a college education, or your own retirement. Many of us spend 10 dollars here and 20 dollars there on frivolous, silly items that we get bored of or throw out months, even weeks later. Chapter 2, **Establishing Your Goals**, discussed the importance of financial goals. Keep these goals in mind when you shop. While it is easier to live for today than it is to plan for tomorrow, purchasing with foresight will help you get to a financially stable future.

Emotional Spending

Have you ever had a bad day and capped it off with a trip to the shopping mall? If so, you are not alone. Many people indulge in such "retail therapy." Treating yourself to something special can seem to take the edge off a particularly rough week. But overindulging in this type of spending can also lead to financial catastrophe. Shopping while bored, stressed, or depressed can cause you to waste your hard-earned cash. As with other forms of impulse buying, ask yourself if you really need the item. The next time you head to the nearest mall, stop and ask yourself what your motivation for shopping is.

To become financially stable, it is likely you will need to make changes to your spending habits. Sensible spending does not mean you should hold off from purchasing necessities or even that you stop buying gifts and going out to lunch. Simply become more mindful of the way you spend your money. If you cut out (or cut down on) unnecessary purchases, you have many options for what to do with your extra money. You might contribute to a long-term savings or retirement account, pay off your credit-card debt, or save it for a special occasion. The benefits gained by spending money wisely are well worth the effort.

WORKSHEETS IN THIS CHAPTER:

· **Monthly Budget Worksheet**: This worksheet allows you to detail your anticipated monthly expenses for the year, including variable, fixed, and installment expenses. Filling out this worksheet to the best of your ability will help you anticipate your expenses as they vary from month to month. For instance, you may anticipate an increase in spending on gifts during the holiday months, or an increase in entertainment expenses during the summer months when your children are out of school. Budgeting for each month also allows you to plan for reserve savings, for unexpected medical bills or car repairs, for instance. Once you have your **Monthly Budget Worksheet** completed, you can refer back to it each month and compare your actual spending with your anticipated expenses.

· **Actual Monthly Expense Worksheet**: Completing each of these 12 worksheets monthly will help you keep track of your bills and fixed expenses, in addition to those expenses that sometimes slip through the cracks and can throw off a budget. These might include a fitness class, dining out, or a shopping trip. At the end of each month, compare your total expenses back to your budget, to see how you did. By keeping track of your monthly spending as it relates to your take-home pay (your income after taxes and withholdings), you can get an accurate assessment of where you are spending wisely or overspending, as well as the areas in which you might be able to cut back to save money.

· **Year At A Glance: Savings Worksheet**: Fill in this worksheet to see how much money you have saved for the entire year.

· **Variable Expenses Annual Summary Worksheet**: Use this yearly expense chart to compare your variable spending month to month.

· **Fixed Expenses Annual Summary Worksheet**: Use this yearly expense chart to compare your fixed spending month to month.

· **Installment Expenses & Net Income Annual Summary Worksheets**: Use the yearly expense chart to compare your installment spending month to month. Next, use the **Net Income Worksheet** to record your salary, bonuses, items sold, tax refunds, and other forms of income accrued throughout the year.

- **Windfall Allocation Worksheet**: Use this worksheet to distribute a lump sum of money, such as a tax refund, inheritance, bonus, or cash gift. It is important to prioritize how you will spend this money; for instance, you may have credit-card debt or a loan to pay off, before you consider a home-improvement project.

- **Credit Card Purchase Worksheet**: Use these quarterly worksheets to keep a record of your credit card purchases. People often make the mistake of overspending on their credit cards, because the bills don't come until many weeks later. Writing down the charges on your credit card helps you avoid impulsive buying.

- **Monthly Bill-Pay Worksheet**: These quarterly worksheets give you space to record your monthly bills as they come in — what you owe and to whom, the dates they are due, and a column to write a checkmark when each bill is paid. This sheet ensures that you will never forget about another bill or miss a due date. As you will learn in the chapter about credit, paying bills promptly is a huge contributor to your credit score.

MONTHLY BUDGET WORKSHEET (SAMPLE)

		January	February	March	April	May	June
	Expected Monthly Income	$ 3,000	$ 3,000	$ 3,000	$	$	$
Expenses							
VARIABLE EXPENSES	Savings	$	$ 100	$	$	$	$
	Investments	$	$	$	$	$	$
	Taxes	$ 500	$ 500	$ 500	$	$	$
	Housing Upkeep	$ 100	$	$	$	$	$
	Food	$ 250	$ 250	$ 250	$	$	$
	Clothing	$	$ 50	$ 50	$	$	$
	Transport	$ 50	$ 50	$ 50	$	$	$
	Personal Care	$ 50	$ 50	$ 50	$	$	$
	Child Expenses	$	$	$	$	$	$
	Health Care	$ 100	$ 100	$ 100	$	$	$
	Education	$	$	$	$	$	$
	Entertainment/Leisure	$ 100	$ 100	$ 100	$	$	$
	Charity	$	$	$	$	$	$
	Other:	$	$	$ 60	$	$	$
FIXED EXPENSES	Rent	$ 1,000	$ 1,000	$ 1,000	$	$	$
	Association Fees	$	$	$	$	$	$
	Property taxes	$	$	$	$	$	$
	Other taxes	$	$	$	$	$	$
	Utilities	$	$ 50	$	$	$	$
	Cable/Satellite TV	$	$	$	$	$	$
	Internet	$ 60	$ 60	$ 60	$	$	$
	Telephone	$ 50	$ 50	$ 50	$	$	$
	Child support	$	$	$	$	$	$
	Spousal support	$	$	$	$	$	$
	Gym	$ 30	$ 30	$ 30	$	$	$
	Home Insurance	$	$	$	$	$	$
	Auto Insurance	$	$	$	$	$	$
	Life Insurance	$	$	$	$	$	$
	Health Insurance	$ 70	$ 70	$ 70	$	$	$
	Dental	$ 30	$ 30	$ 30	$	$	$
	Other:	$	$	$	$	$	$
INSTALLMENT EXPENSES	Credit Card 1	$	$	$	$	$	$
	Credit Card 2	$ 400	$ 400	$ 400	$	$	$
	Credit Card 3	$	$	$	$	$	$
	Loan	$ 100	$ 100	$ 100	$	$	$
	Car payment	$	$	$	$	$	$
	Home mortgage	$	$	$	$	$	$
	Other:	$	$	$	$	$	$
	Total Budget Expenses	$ 2,890	$ 2,990	$ 2,900	$	$	$
	Income - Expenses	$ 110	$ 10	$ 100	$	$	$

SAMPLE

	July	August	September	October	November	December
Expected Monthly Income	$	$	$	$	$	$

Expenses

		July	August	September	October	November	December
VARIABLE EXPENSES	Savings	$	$	$	$	$	$
	Investments	$	$	$	$	$	$
	Taxes	$	$	$	$	$	$
	Housing Upkeep	$	$	$	$	$	$
	Food	$	$	$	$	$	$
	Clothing	$	$	$	$	$	$
	Transport	$	$	$	$	$	$
	Personal Care	$	$	$	$	$	$
	Child Expenses	$	$	$	$	$	$
	Health Care	$	$	$	$	$	$
	Education	$	$	$	$	$	$
	Entertainment/Leisure	$	$	$	$	$	$
	Charity	$	$	$	$	$	$
	Other:	$	$	$	$	$	$
FIXED EXPENSES	Rent	$	$	$	$	$	$
	Association Fees	$	$	$	$	$	$
	Property taxes	$	$	SAMPLE		$	$
	Other taxes	$	$			$	$
	Utilities	$	$	$	$	$	$
	Cable/Satellite TV	$	$	$	$	$	$
	Internet	$	$	$	$	$	$
	Telephone	$	$	$	$	$	$
	Child support	$	$	$	$	$	$
	Spousal support	$	$	$	$	$	$
	Gym	$	$	$	$	$	$
	Home Insurance	$	$	$	$	$	$
	Auto Insurance	$	$	$	$	$	$
	Life Insurance	$	$	$	$	$	$
	Health Insurance	$	$	$	$	$	$
	Dental	$	$	$	$	$	$
	Other:	$	$	$	$	$	$
INSTALLMENT EXPENSES	Credit Card 1	$	$	$	$	$	$
	Credit Card 2	$	$	$	$	$	$
	Credit Card 3	$	$	$	$	$	$
	Loan	$	$	$	$	$	$
	Car payment	$	$	$	$	$	$
	Home mortgage	$	$	$	$	$	$
	Other:	$	$	$	$	$	$
	Total Budget Expenses	$	$	$	$	$	$
	Income - Expenses	$	$	$	$	$	$

MONTHLY BUDGET WORKSHEET

		January	February	March	April	May	June
	Expected Monthly Income	$	$	$	$	$	$
	Expenses						
VARIABLE EXPENSES	Savings	$	$	$	$	$	$
	Investments	$	$	$	$	$	$
	Taxes	$	$	$	$	$	$
	Housing Upkeep	$	$	$	$	$	$
	Food	$	$	$	$	$	$
	Clothing	$	$	$	$	$	$
	Transport	$	$	$	$	$	$
	Personal Care	$	$	$	$	$	$
	Child Expenses	$	$	$	$	$	$
	Health Care	$	$	$	$	$	$
	Education	$	$	$	$	$	$
	Entertainment/Leisure	$	$	$	$	$	$
	Charity	$	$	$	$	$	$
	Other:	$	$	$	$	$	$
FIXED EXPENSES	Rent	$	$	$	$	$	$
	Association Fees	$	$	$	$	$	$
	Property taxes	$	$	$	$	$	$
	Other taxes	$	$	$	$	$	$
	Utilities	$	$	$	$	$	$
	Cable/Satellite TV	$	$	$	$	$	$
	Internet	$	$	$	$	$	$
	Telephone	$	$	$	$	$	$
	Child support	$	$	$	$	$	$
	Spousal support	$	$	$	$	$	$
	Gym	$	$	$	$	$	$
	Home Insurance	$	$	$	$	$	$
	Auto Insurance	$	$	$	$	$	$
	Life Insurance	$	$	$	$	$	$
	Health Insurance	$	$	$	$	$	$
	Dental	$	$	$	$	$	$
	Other:	$	$	$	$	$	$
INSTALLMENT EXPENSES	Credit Card 1	$	$	$	$	$	$
	Credit Card 2	$	$	$	$	$	$
	Credit Card 3	$	$	$	$	$	$
	Loan	$	$	$	$	$	$
	Car payment	$	$	$	$	$	$
	Home mortgage	$	$	$	$	$	$
	Other:	$	$	$	$	$	$
	Total Budget Expenses	$	$	$	$	$	$
	Income - Expenses	$	$	$	$	$	$

		July	August	September	October	November	December
	Expected Monthly Income	$	$	$	$	$	$
Expenses							
VARIABLE EXPENSES	Savings	$	$	$	$	$	$
	Investments	$	$	$	$	$	$
	Taxes	$	$	$	$	$	$
	Housing Upkeep	$	$	$	$	$	$
	Food	$	$	$	$	$	$
	Clothing	$	$	$	$	$	$
	Transport	$	$	$	$	$	$
	Personal Care	$	$	$	$	$	$
	Child Expenses	$	$	$	$	$	$
	Health Care	$	$	$	$	$	$
	Education	$	$	$	$	$	$
	Entertainment/Leisure	$	$	$	$	$	$
	Charity	$	$	$	$	$	$
	Other:	$	$	$	$	$	$
FIXED EXPENSES	Rent	$	$	$	$	$	$
	Association Fees	$	$	$	$	$	$
	Property taxes	$	$	$	$	$	$
	Other taxes	$	$	$	$	$	$
	Utilities	$	$	$	$	$	$
	Cable/Satellite TV	$	$	$	$	$	$
	Internet	$	$	$	$	$	$
	Telephone	$	$	$	$	$	$
	Child support	$	$	$	$	$	$
	Spousal support	$	$	$	$	$	$
	Gym	$	$	$	$	$	$
	Home Insurance	$	$	$	$	$	$
	Auto Insurance	$	$	$	$	$	$
	Life Insurance	$	$	$	$	$	$
	Health Insurance	$	$	$	$	$	$
	Dental	$	$	$	$	$	$
	Other:	$	$	$	$	$	$
INSTALLMENT EXPENSES	Credit Card 1	$	$	$	$	$	$
	Credit Card 2	$	$	$	$	$	$
	Credit Card 3	$	$	$	$	$	$
	Loan	$	$	$	$	$	$
	Car payment	$	$	$	$	$	$
	Home mortgage	$	$	$	$	$	$
	Other:	$	$	$	$	$	$
	Total Budget Expenses	$	$	$	$	$	$
	Income - Expenses	$	$	$	$	$	$

ACTUAL MONTHLY EXPENSE WORKSHEET (SAMPLE)   Month: January   Year: 2009

Net Income:

Balance from previous month	400
Primary Salary/Commissions*	3,000
Secondary Salary/Commissions*	
Bonus	
Dividends, interest, appreciation	
Item(s) sold (car, vacuum, etc.)	
Other income (tax refund, tips, etc.)	
Grand Total Income	3,400

Installment Expenses:

Credit Card 1	300
Credit Card 2	
Credit Card 3	
Loan	100
Car payment	300
Home mortgage	
Other:	
Total Installment Expenses	700

Variable Expenses:

	Savings (Bank account, money market fund, etc.)	Investments (CDs, stocks, funds, bonds, etc.)	Taxes (SS, federal, state, local, etc.)	Housing Upkeep (Repairs, furniture, etc.)	Food (Groceries, restaurants, etc.)	Clothing	Transport (Car service, bus/cab fares, gasoline, etc.)	Personal Care (Haircut, cosmetics, etc.)	Child Expenses (School, toys, etc.)
Day 1									
Day 2									
Day 3									
Day 4					20				
Day 5									
Day 6									
Day 7					20				
Day 8								75	
Day 9									
Day 10					20	50			
Day 11					10				
Day 12					10				
Day 13									
Day 14									
Day 15									
Day 16	200		500	50					
Day 17									
Day 18									
Day 19									
Day 20					20				
Day 21					20				
Day 22									
Day 23									
Day 24					80				
Day 25									
Day 26									
Day 27									
Day 28									
Day 29									
Day 30									
Day 31									
Totals	200		500	50	200	50		75	

* Write your income tax, retirement withholdings and other deductions on the Net Income Annual Summary Worksheet.

Fixed Expenses:

Rent	1,000	Telephone	60	Gym	30	
Association fees		Gas	20	Home Insurance		
Property taxes		Electric	40	Auto Insurance		
Other taxes		Water	30	Life Insurance		
Cable/Satellite TV		Waste disposal		Health Insurance	100	
Internet	50	Child support		Dental	30	
Subscriptions		Spousal support		Other:		
Total	1,050	Total	150	Total	160	

Total Fixed Expenses	1,360

Variable Expenses (continued):

	Health Care (Doctor visits, therapy, medicines, etc.)	Education (Tuition, learning materials, etc.)	Leisure (Movies, travel, etc.)	Gifts (Holidays, birthdays, etc.)	Charity (Donations, contributions, etc.)	Other
Day 1						
Day 2						
Day 3						
Day 4						
Day 5						
Day 6						
Day 7						
Day 8						
Day 9						
Day 10						
Day 11						
Day 12			20			
Day 13						
Day 14						
Day 15						
Day 16						
Day 17						
Day 18						
Day 19			30			
Day 20						
Day 21						
Day 22						
Day 23						
Day 24	20					
Day 25						
Day 26						
Day 27						
Day 28						
Day 29						
Day 30						
Day 31						
Totals	20		50			

Grand Total Expenses:

Total Installment Expenses	700
Total Variable Expenses	1,145
Total Fixed Expenses	1,360
Grand Total Expenses	3,205

Monthly Balance Report:

Grand Total Income	3,400
Grand Total Expenses	3,205
Monthly Balance	195

Monthly Notes:

I should start bringing my lunch to work.

Total Variable Expenses	1,145

ACTUAL MONTHLY EXPENSE WORKSHEET

Month: Year:

Net Income:

Balance from previous month	
Primary Salary/Commissions*	
Secondary Salary/Commissions*	
Bonus	
Dividends, interest, appreciation	
Item(s) sold (car, vacuum, etc.)	
Other income (tax refund, tips, etc.)	
Grand Total Income	

Installment Expenses:

Credit Card 1	
Credit Card 2	
Credit Card 3	
Loan	
Car payment	
Home mortgage	
Other:	
Total Installment Expenses	

Variable Expenses:

	Savings (Bank account, money market fund, etc.)	Investments (CDs, stocks, funds, bonds, etc.)	Taxes (SS, federal, state, local, etc.)	Housing Upkeep (Repairs, furniture, etc.)	Food (Groceries, restaurants, etc.)	Clothing	Transport (Car service, bus/cab fares, gasoline, etc.)	Personal Care (Haircut, cosmetics, etc.)	Child Expenses (School, toys, etc.)
Day 1									
Day 2									
Day 3									
Day 4									
Day 5									
Day 6									
Day 7									
Day 8									
Day 9									
Day 10									
Day 11									
Day 12									
Day 13									
Day 14									
Day 15									
Day 16									
Day 17									
Day 18									
Day 19									
Day 20									
Day 21									
Day 22									
Day 23									
Day 24									
Day 25									
Day 26									
Day 27									
Day 28									
Day 29									
Day 30									
Day 31									
Totals									

* Write your income tax, retirement withholdings and other deductions on the *Net Income Annual Summary Worksheet*.

Fixed Expenses:

Rent		Telephone		Gym	
Association fees		Gas		Home Insurance	
Property taxes		Electric		Auto Insurance	
Other taxes		Water		Life Insurance	
Cable/Satellite TV		Waste disposal		Health Insurance	
Internet		Child support		Dental	
Subscriptions		Spousal support		Other:	
Total		Total		Total	

Total Fixed Expenses	

Variable Expenses (continued):

	Health Care (Doctor visits, therapy, medicines, etc.)	Education (Tuition, learning materials, etc.)	Leisure (Movies, travel, etc.)	Gifts (Holidays, birthdays, etc.)	Charity (Donations, contributions, etc.)	Other
Day 1						
Day 2						
Day 3						
Day 4						
Day 5						
Day 6						
Day 7						
Day 8						
Day 9						
Day 10						
Day 11						
Day 12						
Day 13						
Day 14						
Day 15						
Day 16						
Day 17						
Day 18						
Day 19						
Day 20						
Day 21						
Day 22						
Day 23						
Day 24						
Day 25						
Day 26						
Day 27						
Day 28						
Day 29						
Day 30						
Day 31						
Totals						

Grand Total Expenses:

Total Installment Expenses	
Total Variable Expenses	
Total Fixed Expenses	
Grand Total Expenses	

Monthly Balance Report:

Grand Total Income	
Grand Total Expenses	
Monthly Balance	

Monthly Notes:

Total Variable Expenses	

ACTUAL MONTHLY EXPENSE WORKSHEET

Month: _____ Year: _____

Net Income:

Balance from previous month	
Primary Salary/Commissions*	
Secondary Salary/Commissions*	
Bonus	
Dividends, interest, appreciation	
Item(s) sold (car, vacuum, etc.)	
Other income (tax refund, tips, etc.)	
Grand Total Income	

Installment Expenses:

Credit Card 1	
Credit Card 2	
Credit Card 3	
Loan	
Car payment	
Home mortgage	
Other:	
Total Installment Expenses	

Variable Expenses:

	Savings (Bank account, money market fund, etc.)	Investments (CDs, stocks, funds, bonds, etc.)	Taxes (SS, federal, state, local, etc.)	Housing Upkeep (Repairs, furniture, etc.)	Food (Groceries, restaurants, etc.)	Clothing	Transport (Car service, bus/cab fares, gasoline, etc.)	Personal Care (Haircut, cosmetics, etc.)	Child Expenses (School, toys, etc.)
Day 1									
Day 2									
Day 3									
Day 4									
Day 5									
Day 6									
Day 7									
Day 8									
Day 9									
Day 10									
Day 11									
Day 12									
Day 13									
Day 14									
Day 15									
Day 16									
Day 17									
Day 18									
Day 19									
Day 20									
Day 21									
Day 22									
Day 23									
Day 24									
Day 25									
Day 26									
Day 27									
Day 28									
Day 29									
Day 30									
Day 31									
Totals									

* Write your income tax, retirement withholdings and other deductions on the *Net Income Annual Summary Worksheet.*

Fixed Expenses:

Rent		Telephone		Gym	
Association fees		Gas		Home Insurance	
Property taxes		Electric		Auto Insurance	
Other taxes		Water		Life Insurance	
Cable/Satellite TV		Waste disposal		Health Insurance	
Internet		Child support		Dental	
Subscriptions		Spousal support		Other:	
Total		Total		Total	

Total Fixed Expenses	

Variable Expenses (continued):

	Health Care (Doctor visits, therapy, medicines, etc.)	Education (Tuition, learning materials, etc.)	Leisure (Movies, travel, etc.)	Gifts (Holidays, birthdays, etc.)	Charity (Donations, contributions, etc.)	Other
Day 1						
Day 2						
Day 3						
Day 4						
Day 5						
Day 6						
Day 7						
Day 8						
Day 9						
Day 10						
Day 11						
Day 12						
Day 13						
Day 14						
Day 15						
Day 16						
Day 17						
Day 18						
Day 19						
Day 20						
Day 21						
Day 22						
Day 23						
Day 24						
Day 25						
Day 26						
Day 27						
Day 28						
Day 29						
Day 30						
Day 31						
Totals						

Total Variable Expenses	

Grand Total Expenses:

Total Installment Expenses	
Total Variable Expenses	
Total Fixed Expenses	
Grand Total Expenses	

Monthly Balance Report:

Grand Total Income	
Grand Total Expenses	
Monthly Balance	

Monthly Notes:

_____

_____

_____

_____

_____

_____

_____

_____

_____

_____

_____

_____

ACTUAL MONTHLY EXPENSE WORKSHEET

Month: _____ Year: _____

Net Income:

Balance from previous month	
Primary Salary/Commissions*	
Secondary Salary/Commissions*	
Bonus	
Dividends, interest, appreciation	
Item(s) sold (car, vacuum, etc.)	
Other income (tax refund, tips, etc.)	
Grand Total Income	

Installment Expenses:

Credit Card 1	
Credit Card 2	
Credit Card 3	
Loan	
Car payment	
Home mortgage	
Other:	
Total Installment Expenses	

Variable Expenses:

	Savings (Bank account, money market fund, etc.)	Investments (CDs, stocks, funds, bonds, etc.)	Taxes (SS, federal, state, local, etc.)	Housing Upkeep (Repairs, furniture, etc.)	Food (Groceries, restaurants, etc.)	Clothing	Transport (Car service, bus/cab fares, gasoline, etc.)	Personal Care (Haircut, cosmetics, etc.)	Child Expenses (School, toys, etc.)
Day 1									
Day 2									
Day 3									
Day 4									
Day 5									
Day 6									
Day 7									
Day 8									
Day 9									
Day 10									
Day 11									
Day 12									
Day 13									
Day 14									
Day 15									
Day 16									
Day 17									
Day 18									
Day 19									
Day 20									
Day 21									
Day 22									
Day 23									
Day 24									
Day 25									
Day 26									
Day 27									
Day 28									
Day 29									
Day 30									
Day 31									
Totals									

* Write your income tax, retirement withholdings and other deductions on the *Net Income Annual Summary Worksheet.*

Fixed Expenses:

Rent		Telephone		Gym			
Association fees		Gas		Home Insurance			
Property taxes		Electric		Auto Insurance			
Other taxes		Water		Life Insurance			
Cable/Satellite TV		Waste disposal		Health Insurance			
Internet		Child support		Dental			
Subscriptions		Spousal support		Other:		Total Fixed Expenses	
Total		Total		Total			

Variable Expenses (continued):

	Health Care (Doctor visits, therapy, medicines, etc.)	Education (Tuition, learning materials, etc.)	Leisure (Movies, travel, etc.)	Gifts (Holidays, birthdays, etc.)	Charity (Donations, contributions, etc.)	Other
Day 1						
Day 2						
Day 3						
Day 4						
Day 5						
Day 6						
Day 7						
Day 8						
Day 9						
Day 10						
Day 11						
Day 12						
Day 13						
Day 14						
Day 15						
Day 16						
Day 17						
Day 18						
Day 19						
Day 20						
Day 21						
Day 22						
Day 23						
Day 24						
Day 25						
Day 26						
Day 27						
Day 28						
Day 29						
Day 30						
Day 31						
Totals						

Grand Total Expenses:

Total Installment Expenses	
Total Variable Expenses	
Total Fixed Expenses	
Grand Total Expenses	

Monthly Balance Report:

Grand Total Income	
Grand Total Expenses	
Monthly Balance	

Monthly Notes:

Total Variable Expenses

ACTUAL MONTHLY EXPENSE WORKSHEET

Month: Year:

Net Income:

Balance from previous month	
Primary Salary/Commissions*	
Secondary Salary/Commissions*	
Bonus	
Dividends, interest, appreciation	
Item(s) sold (car, vacuum, etc.)	
Other income (tax refund, tips, etc.)	
Grand Total Income	

Installment Expenses:

Credit Card 1	
Credit Card 2	
Credit Card 3	
Loan	
Car payment	
Home mortgage	
Other:	
Total Installment Expenses	

Variable Expenses:

	Savings (Bank account, money market fund, etc.)	Investments (CDs, stocks, funds, bonds, etc.)	Taxes (SS, federal, state, local, etc.)	Housing Upkeep (Repairs, furniture, etc.)	Food (Groceries, restaurants, etc.)	Clothing	Transport (Car service, bus/cab fares, gasoline, etc.)	Personal Care (Haircut, cosmetics, etc.)	Child Expenses (School, toys, etc.)
Day 1									
Day 2									
Day 3									
Day 4									
Day 5									
Day 6									
Day 7									
Day 8									
Day 9									
Day 10									
Day 11									
Day 12									
Day 13									
Day 14									
Day 15									
Day 16									
Day 17									
Day 18									
Day 19									
Day 20									
Day 21									
Day 22									
Day 23									
Day 24									
Day 25									
Day 26									
Day 27									
Day 28									
Day 29									
Day 30									
Day 31									
Totals									

* Write your income tax, retirement withholdings and other deductions on the *Net Income Annual Summary Worksheet.*

Fixed Expenses:

Rent		Telephone		Gym		
Association fees		Gas		Home Insurance		
Property taxes		Electric		Auto Insurance		
Other taxes		Water		Life Insurance		
Cable/Satellite TV		Waste disposal		Health Insurance		
Internet		Child support		Dental		
Subscriptions		Spousal support		Other:		**Total Fixed Expenses**
Total		**Total**		**Total**		

Variable Expenses (continued):

	Health Care (Doctor visits, therapy, medicines, etc.)	Education (Tuition, learning materials, etc.)	Leisure (Movies, travel, etc.)	Gifts (Holidays, birthdays, etc.)	Charity (Donations, contributions, etc.)	Other
Day 1						
Day 2						
Day 3						
Day 4						
Day 5						
Day 6						
Day 7						
Day 8						
Day 9						
Day 10						
Day 11						
Day 12						
Day 13						
Day 14						
Day 15						
Day 16						
Day 17						
Day 18						
Day 19						
Day 20						
Day 21						
Day 22						
Day 23						
Day 24						
Day 25						
Day 26						
Day 27						
Day 28						
Day 29						
Day 30						
Day 31						
Totals						

Grand Total Expenses:

Total Installment Expenses	
Total Variable Expenses	
Total Fixed Expenses	
Grand Total Expenses	

Monthly Balance Report:

Grand Total Income	
Grand Total Expenses	
Monthly Balance	

Monthly Notes:

_____

_____

_____

_____

_____

_____

_____

_____

_____

_____

_____

Total Variable Expenses	

ACTUAL MONTHLY EXPENSE WORKSHEET

Month: _____   Year: _____

Net Income:

Balance from previous month	
Primary Salary/Commissions*	
Secondary Salary/Commissions*	
Bonus	
Dividends, interest, appreciation	
Item(s) sold (car, vacuum, etc.)	
Other income (tax refund, tips, etc.)	
Grand Total Income	

Installment Expenses:

Credit Card 1	
Credit Card 2	
Credit Card 3	
Loan	
Car payment	
Home mortgage	
Other:	
Total Installment Expenses	

Variable Expenses:

	Savings (Bank account, money market fund, etc.)	Investments (CDs, stocks, funds, bonds, etc.)	Taxes (SS, federal, state, local, etc.)	Housing Upkeep (Repairs, furniture, etc.)	Food (Groceries, restaurants, etc.)	Clothing	Transport (Car service, bus/cab fares, gasoline, etc.)	Personal Care (Haircut, cosmetics, etc.)	Child Expenses (School, toys, etc.)
Day 1									
Day 2									
Day 3									
Day 4									
Day 5									
Day 6									
Day 7									
Day 8									
Day 9									
Day 10									
Day 11									
Day 12									
Day 13									
Day 14									
Day 15									
Day 16									
Day 17									
Day 18									
Day 19									
Day 20									
Day 21									
Day 22									
Day 23									
Day 24									
Day 25									
Day 26									
Day 27									
Day 28									
Day 29									
Day 30									
Day 31									
Totals									

*Write your income tax, retirement withholdings and other deductions on the Net Income Annual Summary Worksheet.

Fixed Expenses:

Rent		Telephone		Gym		
Association fees		Gas		Home Insurance		
Property taxes		Electric		Auto Insurance		
Other taxes		Water		Life Insurance		
Cable/Satellite TV		Waste disposal		Health Insurance		
Internet		Child support		Dental		
Subscriptions		Spousal support		Other:		
Total		Total		Total		Total Fixed Expenses

Variable Expenses (continued):

	Health Care (Doctor visits, therapy, medicines, etc.)	Education (Tuition, learning materials, etc.)	Leisure (Movies, travel, etc.)	Gifts (Holidays, birthdays, etc.)	Charity (Donations, contributions, etc.)	Other
Day 1						
Day 2						
Day 3						
Day 4						
Day 5						
Day 6						
Day 7						
Day 8						
Day 9						
Day 10						
Day 11						
Day 12						
Day 13						
Day 14						
Day 15						
Day 16						
Day 17						
Day 18						
Day 19						
Day 20						
Day 21						
Day 22						
Day 23						
Day 24						
Day 25						
Day 26						
Day 27						
Day 28						
Day 29						
Day 30						
Day 31						
Totals						

Grand Total Expenses:

Total Installment Expenses	
Total Variable Expenses	
Total Fixed Expenses	
Grand Total Expenses	

Monthly Balance Report:

Grand Total Income	
Grand Total Expenses	
Monthly Balance	

Monthly Notes:

Total Variable Expenses

ACTUAL MONTHLY EXPENSE WORKSHEET   Month: Year:

Net Income:

Balance from previous month	
Primary Salary/Commissions*	
Secondary Salary/Commissions*	
Bonus	
Dividends, interest, appreciation	
Item(s) sold (car, vacuum, etc.)	
Other income (tax refund, tips, etc.)	
Grand Total Income	

Installment Expenses:

Credit Card 1	
Credit Card 2	
Credit Card 3	
Loan	
Car payment	
Home mortgage	
Other:	
Total Installment Expenses	

Variable Expenses:

	Savings (Bank account, money market fund, etc.)	Investments (CDs, stocks, funds, bonds, etc.)	Taxes (SS, federal, state, local, etc.)	Housing Upkeep (Repairs, furniture, etc.)	Food (Groceries, restaurants, etc.)	Clothing	Transport (Car service, bus/cab fares, gasoline, etc.)	Personal Care (Haircut, cosmetics, etc.)	Child Expenses (School, toys, etc.)
Day 1									
Day 2									
Day 3									
Day 4									
Day 5									
Day 6									
Day 7									
Day 8									
Day 9									
Day 10									
Day 11									
Day 12									
Day 13									
Day 14									
Day 15									
Day 16									
Day 17									
Day 18									
Day 19									
Day 20									
Day 21									
Day 22									
Day 23									
Day 24									
Day 25									
Day 26									
Day 27									
Day 28									
Day 29									
Day 30									
Day 31									
Totals									

*Write your income tax, retirement withholdings and other deductions on the *Net Income Annual Summary Worksheet*.

Fixed Expenses:

Rent		Telephone		Gym	
Association fees		Gas		Home Insurance	
Property taxes		Electric		Auto Insurance	
Other taxes		Water		Life Insurance	
Cable/Satellite TV		Waste disposal		Health Insurance	
Internet		Child support		Dental	
Subscriptions		Spousal support		Other:	
Total		Total		Total	

Total Fixed Expenses	

Variable Expenses (continued):

	Health Care (Doctor visits, therapy, medicines, etc.)	Education (Tuition, learning materials, etc.)	Leisure (Movies, travel, etc.)	Gifts (Holidays, birthdays, etc.)	Charity (Donations, contributions, etc.)	Other
Day 1						
Day 2						
Day 3						
Day 4						
Day 5						
Day 6						
Day 7						
Day 8						
Day 9						
Day 10						
Day 11						
Day 12						
Day 13						
Day 14						
Day 15						
Day 16						
Day 17						
Day 18						
Day 19						
Day 20						
Day 21						
Day 22						
Day 23						
Day 24						
Day 25						
Day 26						
Day 27						
Day 28						
Day 29						
Day 30						
Day 31						
Totals						

Grand Total Expenses:

Total Installment Expenses	
Total Variable Expenses	
Total Fixed Expenses	
Grand Total Expenses	

Monthly Balance Report:

Grand Total Income	
Grand Total Expenses	
Monthly Balance	

Monthly Notes:

_____

_____

_____

_____

_____

_____

_____

_____

_____

_____

_____

Total Variable Expenses	

ACTUAL MONTHLY EXPENSE WORKSHEET

Month: Year:

Net Income:

Balance from previous month	
Primary Salary/Commissions*	
Secondary Salary/Commissions*	
Bonus	
Dividends, interest, appreciation	
Item(s) sold (car, vacuum, etc.)	
Other income (tax refund, tips, etc.)	
Grand Total Income	

Installment Expenses:

Credit Card 1	
Credit Card 2	
Credit Card 3	
Loan	
Car payment	
Home mortgage	
Other:	
Total Installment Expenses	

Variable Expenses:

	Savings (Bank account, money market fund, etc.)	Investments (CDs, stocks, funds, bonds, etc.)	Taxes (SS, federal, state, local, etc.)	Housing Upkeep (Repairs, furniture, etc.)	Food (Groceries, restaurants, etc.)	Clothing	Transport (Car service, bus/cab fares, gasoline, etc.)	Personal Care (Haircut, cosmetics, etc.)	Child Expenses (School, toys, etc.)
Day 1									
Day 2									
Day 3									
Day 4									
Day 5									
Day 6									
Day 7									
Day 8									
Day 9									
Day 10									
Day 11									
Day 12									
Day 13									
Day 14									
Day 15									
Day 16									
Day 17									
Day 18									
Day 19									
Day 20									
Day 21									
Day 22									
Day 23									
Day 24									
Day 25									
Day 26									
Day 27									
Day 28									
Day 29									
Day 30									
Day 31									
Totals									

*Write your income tax, retirement withholdings and other deductions on the Net Income Annual Summary Worksheet.

Fixed Expenses:

Rent	
Association fees	
Property taxes	
Other taxes	
Cable/Satellite TV	
Internet	
Subscriptions	
Total	

Telephone	
Gas	
Electric	
Water	
Waste disposal	
Child support	
Spousal support	
Total	

Gym	
Home Insurance	
Auto Insurance	
Life Insurance	
Health Insurance	
Dental	
Other:	
Total	

Total Fixed Expenses	

Variable Expenses (continued):

	Health Care (Doctor visits, therapy, medicines, etc.)	Education (Tuition, learning materials, etc.)	Leisure (Movies, travel, etc.)	Gifts (Holidays, birthdays, etc.)	Charity (Donations, contributions, etc.)	Other
Day 1						
Day 2						
Day 3						
Day 4						
Day 5						
Day 6						
Day 7						
Day 8						
Day 9						
Day 10						
Day 11						
Day 12						
Day 13						
Day 14						
Day 15						
Day 16						
Day 17						
Day 18						
Day 19						
Day 20						
Day 21						
Day 22						
Day 23						
Day 24						
Day 25						
Day 26						
Day 27						
Day 28						
Day 29						
Day 30						
Day 31						
Totals						

Grand Total Expenses:

Total Installment Expenses	
Total Variable Expenses	
Total Fixed Expenses	
Grand Total Expenses	

Monthly Balance Report:

Grand Total Income	
Grand Total Expenses	
Monthly Balance	

Monthly Notes:

_____

_____

_____

_____

_____

_____

_____

_____

_____

_____

_____

_____

_____

Total Variable Expenses	

ACTUAL MONTHLY EXPENSE WORKSHEET

Month: Year:

Net Income:

Balance from previous month	
Primary Salary/Commissions*	
Secondary Salary/Commissions*	
Bonus	
Dividends, interest, appreciation	
Item(s) sold (car, vacuum, etc.)	
Other income (tax refund, tips, etc.)	
Grand Total Income	

Installment Expenses:

Credit Card 1	
Credit Card 2	
Credit Card 3	
Loan	
Car payment	
Home mortgage	
Other:	
Total Installment Expenses	

Variable Expenses:

	Savings (Bank account, money market fund, etc.)	Investments (CDs, stocks, funds, bonds, etc.)	Taxes (SS, federal, state, local, etc.)	Housing Upkeep (Repairs, furniture, etc.)	Food (Groceries, restaurants, etc.)	Clothing	Transport (Car service, bus/cab fares, gasoline, etc.)	Personal Care (Haircut, cosmetics, etc.)	Child Expenses (School, toys, etc.)
Day 1									
Day 2									
Day 3									
Day 4									
Day 5									
Day 6									
Day 7									
Day 8									
Day 9									
Day 10									
Day 11									
Day 12									
Day 13									
Day 14									
Day 15									
Day 16									
Day 17									
Day 18									
Day 19									
Day 20									
Day 21									
Day 22									
Day 23									
Day 24									
Day 25									
Day 26									
Day 27									
Day 28									
Day 29									
Day 30									
Day 31									
Totals									

* Write your income tax, retirement withholdings and other deductions on the *Net Income Annual Summary* Worksheet.

Fixed Expenses:

Rent		Telephone		Gym			
Association fees		Gas		Home Insurance			
Property taxes		Electric		Auto Insurance			
Other taxes		Water		Life Insurance			
Cable/Satellite TV		Waste disposal		Health Insurance			
Internet		Child support		Dental			
Subscriptions		Spousal support		Other:		Total Fixed Expenses	
Total		Total		Total			

Variable Expenses (continued):

	Health Care (Doctor visits, therapy, medicines, etc.)	Education (Tuition, learning materials, etc.)	Leisure (Movies, travel, etc.)	Gifts (Holidays, birthdays, etc.)	Charity (Donations, contributions, etc.)	Other
Day 1						
Day 2						
Day 3						
Day 4						
Day 5						
Day 6						
Day 7						
Day 8						
Day 9						
Day 10						
Day 11						
Day 12						
Day 13						
Day 14						
Day 15						
Day 16						
Day 17						
Day 18						
Day 19						
Day 20						
Day 21						
Day 22						
Day 23						
Day 24						
Day 25						
Day 26						
Day 27						
Day 28						
Day 29						
Day 30						
Day 31						
Totals						

Grand Total Expenses:

Total Installment Expenses	
Total Variable Expenses	
Total Fixed Expenses	
Grand Total Expenses	

Monthly Balance Report:

Grand Total Income	
Grand Total Expenses	
Monthly Balance	

Monthly Notes:

Total Variable Expenses

ACTUAL MONTHLY EXPENSE WORKSHEET

Month: Year:

Net Income:

Balance from previous month	
Primary Salary/Commissions*	
Secondary Salary/Commissions*	
Bonus	
Dividends, interest, appreciation	
Item(s) sold (car, vacuum, etc.)	
Other income (tax refund, tips, etc.)	
Grand Total Income	

Installment Expenses:

Credit Card 1	
Credit Card 2	
Credit Card 3	
Loan	
Car payment	
Home mortgage	
Other:	
Total Installment Expenses	

Variable Expenses:

	Savings (Bank account, money market fund, etc.)	Investments (CDs, stocks, funds, bonds, etc.)	Taxes (SS, federal, state, local, etc.)	Housing Upkeep (Repairs, furniture, etc.)	Food (Groceries, restaurants, etc.)	Clothing	Transport (Car service, bus/cab fares, gasoline, etc.)	Personal Care (Haircut, cosmetics, etc.)	Child Expenses (School, toys, etc.)
Day 1									
Day 2									
Day 3									
Day 4									
Day 5									
Day 6									
Day 7									
Day 8									
Day 9									
Day 10									
Day 11									
Day 12									
Day 13									
Day 14									
Day 15									
Day 16									
Day 17									
Day 18									
Day 19									
Day 20									
Day 21									
Day 22									
Day 23									
Day 24									
Day 25									
Day 26									
Day 27									
Day 28									
Day 29									
Day 30									
Day 31									
Totals									

* Write your income tax, retirement withholdings and other deductions on the *Net Income Annual Summary Worksheet*.

Fixed Expenses:

Rent		Telephone		Gym		
Association fees		Gas		Home Insurance		
Property taxes		Electric		Auto Insurance		
Other taxes		Water		Life Insurance		
Cable/Satellite TV		Waste disposal		Health Insurance		
Internet		Child support		Dental		
Subscriptions		Spousal support		Other:		
Total		Total		Total		

Total Fixed Expenses	

Variable Expenses (continued):

	Health Care (Doctor visits, therapy, medicines, etc.)	Education (Tuition, learning materials, etc.)	Leisure (Movies, travel, etc.)	Gifts (Holidays, birthdays, etc.)	Charity (Donations, contributions, etc.)	Other
Day 1						
Day 2						
Day 3						
Day 4						
Day 5						
Day 6						
Day 7						
Day 8						
Day 9						
Day 10						
Day 11						
Day 12						
Day 13						
Day 14						
Day 15						
Day 16						
Day 17						
Day 18						
Day 19						
Day 20						
Day 21						
Day 22						
Day 23						
Day 24						
Day 25						
Day 26						
Day 27						
Day 28						
Day 29						
Day 30						
Day 31						
Totals						

Total Variable Expenses	

Grand Total Expenses:

Total Installment Expenses	
Total Variable Expenses	
Total Fixed Expenses	
Grand Total Expenses	

Monthly Balance Report:

Grand Total Income	
Grand Total Expenses	
Monthly Balance	

Monthly Notes:

_____

_____

_____

_____

_____

_____

_____

_____

_____

_____

_____

ACTUAL MONTHLY EXPENSE WORKSHEET

Month: _____   Year: _____

Net Income:

Balance from previous month	
Primary Salary/Commissions*	
Secondary Salary/Commissions*	
Bonus	
Dividends, interest, appreciation	
Item(s) sold (car, vacuum, etc.)	
Other income (tax refund, tips, etc.)	
Grand Total Income	

Installment Expenses:

Credit Card 1	
Credit Card 2	
Credit Card 3	
Loan	
Car payment	
Home mortgage	
Other:	
Total Installment Expenses	

Variable Expenses:

	Savings (Bank account, money market fund, etc.)	Investments (CDs, stocks, funds, bonds, etc.)	Taxes (SS, federal, state, local, etc.)	Housing Upkeep (Repairs, furniture, etc.)	Food (Groceries, restaurants, etc.)	Clothing	Transport (Car service, bus/cab fares, gasoline, etc.)	Personal Care (Haircut, cosmetics, etc.)	Child Expenses (School, toys, etc.)
Day 1									
Day 2									
Day 3									
Day 4									
Day 5									
Day 6									
Day 7									
Day 8									
Day 9									
Day 10									
Day 11									
Day 12									
Day 13									
Day 14									
Day 15									
Day 16									
Day 17									
Day 18									
Day 19									
Day 20									
Day 21									
Day 22									
Day 23									
Day 24									
Day 25									
Day 26									
Day 27									
Day 28									
Day 29									
Day 30									
Day 31									
Totals									

* Write your income tax, retirement withholdings and other deductions on the Net Income Annual Summary Worksheet.

Fixed Expenses:

Rent		Telephone		Gym	
Association fees		Gas		Home Insurance	
Property taxes		Electric		Auto Insurance	
Other taxes		Water		Life Insurance	
Cable/Satellite TV		Waste disposal		Health Insurance	
Internet		Child support		Dental	
Subscriptions		Spousal support		Other:	
Total		**Total**		**Total**	

Total Fixed Expenses	

Variable Expenses (continued):

	Health Care (Doctor visits, therapy, medicines, etc.)	Education (Tuition, learning materials, etc.)	Leisure (Movies, travel, etc.)	Gifts (Holidays, birthdays, etc.)	Charity (Donations, contributions, etc.)	Other
Day 1						
Day 2						
Day 3						
Day 4						
Day 5						
Day 6						
Day 7						
Day 8						
Day 9						
Day 10						
Day 11						
Day 12						
Day 13						
Day 14						
Day 15						
Day 16						
Day 17						
Day 18						
Day 19						
Day 20						
Day 21						
Day 22						
Day 23						
Day 24						
Day 25						
Day 26						
Day 27						
Day 28						
Day 29						
Day 30						
Day 31						
Totals						

Grand Total Expenses:

Total Installment Expenses	
Total Variable Expenses	
Total Fixed Expenses	
Grand Total Expenses	

Monthly Balance Report:

Grand Total Income	
Grand Total Expenses	
Monthly Balance	

Monthly Notes:

_____

_____

_____

_____

_____

_____

_____

_____

_____

_____

_____

Total Variable Expenses	

ACTUAL MONTHLY EXPENSE WORKSHEET

Month: Year:

Net Income:

Balance from previous month	
Primary Salary/Commissions*	
Secondary Salary/Commissions*	
Bonus	
Dividends, interest, appreciation	
Item(s) sold (car, vacuum, etc.)	
Other income (tax refund, tips, etc.)	
Grand Total Income	

Installment Expenses:

Credit Card 1	
Credit Card 2	
Credit Card 3	
Loan	
Car payment	
Home mortgage	
Other:	
Total Installment Expenses	

Variable Expenses:

	Savings (Bank account, money market fund, etc.)	Investments (CDs, stocks, funds, bonds, etc.)	Taxes (SS, federal, state, local, etc.)	Housing Upkeep (Repairs, furniture, etc.)	Food (Groceries, restaurants, etc.)	Clothing	Transport (Car service, bus/cab fares, gasoline, etc.)	Personal Care (Haircut, cosmetics, etc.)	Child Expenses (School, toys, etc.)
Day 1									
Day 2									
Day 3									
Day 4									
Day 5									
Day 6									
Day 7									
Day 8									
Day 9									
Day 10									
Day 11									
Day 12									
Day 13									
Day 14									
Day 15									
Day 16									
Day 17									
Day 18									
Day 19									
Day 20									
Day 21									
Day 22									
Day 23									
Day 24									
Day 25									
Day 26									
Day 27									
Day 28									
Day 29									
Day 30									
Day 31									
Totals									

* Write your income tax, retirement withholdings and other deductions on the *Net Income Annual Summary Worksheet.*

Fixed Expenses:

Rent		Telephone		Gym	
Association fees		Gas		Home Insurance	
Property taxes		Electric		Auto Insurance	
Other taxes		Water		Life Insurance	
Cable/Satellite TV		Waste disposal		Health Insurance	
Internet		Child support		Dental	
Subscriptions		Spousal support		Other:	
Total		Total		Total	

Total Fixed Expenses	

Variable Expenses (continued):

	Health Care (Doctor visits, therapy, medicines, etc.)	Education (Tuition, learning materials, etc.)	Leisure (Movies, travel, etc.)	Gifts (Holidays, birthdays, etc.)	Charity (Donations, contributions, etc.)	Other
Day 1						
Day 2						
Day 3						
Day 4						
Day 5						
Day 6						
Day 7						
Day 8						
Day 9						
Day 10						
Day 11						
Day 12						
Day 13						
Day 14						
Day 15						
Day 16						
Day 17						
Day 18						
Day 19						
Day 20						
Day 21						
Day 22						
Day 23						
Day 24						
Day 25						
Day 26						
Day 27						
Day 28						
Day 29						
Day 30						
Day 31						
Totals						

Grand Total Expenses:

Total Installment Expenses	
Total Variable Expenses	
Total Fixed Expenses	
Grand Total Expenses	

Monthly Balance Report:

Grand Total Income	
Grand Total Expenses	
Monthly Balance	

Monthly Notes:

Total Variable Expenses	

	Previous Month Total Savings (A)	Actual Income (B)	Actual Expense (C)	Savings this Month (D) B - C	Total Savings A + D
Jan.	0	3,200	2,600	600	600
Feb.	600	3,350	2,750	600	1,200
March	1,200	3,350	2,675	675	1,875
April	1,875	3,350	2,650	700	2,575
May	2,575	3,350	2,700	650	3,225
June	3,225	3,225	2,900	325	3,550
July	3,550	3,350	2,750	600	4,150
Aug.	4,150	3,225	2,600	625	4,775
Sept.	4,775	3,500	2,400	1,100	5,875
Oct.	5,875	3,500	2,675	825	6,700
Nov.	6,700	3,500	2,520	980	7,680
Dec.	7,680	4,500	2,400	2,100	9,780

▲

Total Savings
for the Year

	Previous Month Total Savings (A)	Actual Income (B)	Actual Expense (C)	Savings this Month (D) B - C	Total Savings A + D
Jan.					
Feb.					
March					
April					
May					
June					
July					
Aug.					
Sept.					
Oct.					
Nov.					
Dec.					

▲

Total Savings
for the Year

VARIABLE EXPENSES ANNUAL SUMMARY WORKSHEET

	Jan.	Feb.	March	April	May	June	July	Aug.	Sept.	Oct.	Nov.	Dec.	Year Totals	Mo. Avg.
Savings														
Investments														
Taxes														
Housing Upkeep														
Food														
Clothing														
Transport														
Personal Care														
Child Expenses														
Health Care														
Education														
Leisure														
Gifts														
Charity														
Other														

Total Annual Variable Expenses
(Sum of all Year Totals)

FIXED EXPENSES ANNUAL SUMMARY WORKSHEET

	Jan.	Feb.	March	April	May	June	July	Aug.	Sept.	Oct.	Nov.	Dec.	Year Totals	Mo. Avg.
Rent														
HOA Fees														
Property taxes														
Other taxes														
TV (cable/satellite)														
Internet														
Subscriptions														
Telephone														
Gas														
Electric														
Water														
Waste disposal														
Child support														
Spousal support														
Gym														
Home Insurance														
Auto Insurance														
Life Insurance														
Health Insurance														
Dental														
Other														

Total Annual Fixed Expenses
(Sum of all Year Totals)

INSTALLMENT EXPENSES & NET INCOME ANNUAL SUMMARY WORKSHEETS

Installment Expenses:

	Jan.	Feb.	March	April	May	June	July	Aug.	Sept.	Oct.	Nov.	Dec.	Year Totals	Mo. Avg.
Credit Card 1														
Credit Card 2														
Credit Card 3														
Loan														
Car payment														
Home mortgage														
Other:														

Total Annual Installment Expenses
(Sum of all Year Totals)

Net Income:

	Jan.	Feb.	March	April	May	June	July	Aug.	Sept.	Oct.	Nov.	Dec.	Year Totals	Mo. Avg.
Balance from previous month														
Primary Salary														
Secondary Salary														
Dividends, interest, etc.														
Item(s) sold (car, vacuum, etc.)														
Bonus														
Other income (tax refund, tips, etc.)														

Total Annual Net Income
(Sum of all Year Totals)

Date:

Source of money:

Total amount:

Expenses to consider	Amount	Percent
If no taxes have been taken out, estimated amount to pay off taxable sum (put into savings)	$	%
Late payments (bills currently behind on)	$	%
Back taxes	$	%
Credit card #1 to pay off or down:	$	%
Credit card #2 to pay off or down:	$	%
Credit card #3 to pay off or down:	$	%
Loan #1 to pay off or down	$	%
Loan #2 to pay off or down	$	%
Future months of living expenses (put into savings)	$	%
Household supplies and grocery items	$	%
Major future expenses	$	%
Reserve savings account	$	%
Emergency savings account	$	%
Home improvement project(s)	$	%
Investments and/or retirement	$	%
New purchases	$	%
Vacation and/or leisure activities	$	%
Other:	$	%
Other:	$	%
Other:	$	%
Total Windfall Amount	$	%
Total Expenses	$	%
Total Remaining	$	%

JANUARY			FEBRUARY			MARCH		
End of billing cycle:			End of billing cycle:			End of billing cycle:		
Day	Item	Amount	Day	Item	Amount	Day	Item	Amount
Monthly Totals								

APRIL			MAY			JUNE		
End of billing cycle:			End of billing cycle:			End of billing cycle:		
Day	Item	Amount	Day	Item	Amount	Day	Item	Amount
Monthly Totals								

JULY			AUGUST			SEPTEMBER		
End of billing cycle:			End of billing cycle:			End of billing cycle:		
Day	Item	Amount	Day	Item	Amount	Day	Item	Amount
Monthly Totals								

OCTOBER			NOVEMBER			DECEMBER		
End of billing cycle:			End of billing cycle:			End of billing cycle:		
Day	Item	Amount	Day	Item	Amount	Day	Item	Amount
Monthly Totals								

JANUARY				FEBRUARY				MARCH			
Bill	Amount Due	Date Due	Paid	Bill	Amount Due	Date Due	Paid	Bill	Amount Due	Date Due	Paid

APRIL				MAY				JUNE			
Bill	Amount Due	Date Due	Paid	Bill	Amount Due	Date Due	Paid	Bill	Amount Due	Date Due	Paid

JULY				AUGUST				SEPTEMBER			
Bill	Amount Due	Date Due	Paid	Bill	Amount Due	Date Due	Paid	Bill	Amount Due	Date Due	Paid

OCTOBER				NOVEMBER				DECEMBER			
Bill	Amount Due	Date Due	Paid	Bill	Amount Due	Date Due	Paid	Bill	Amount Due	Date Due	Paid

WAYS TO SAVE MONEY

Once you've assessed your financial situation, established your goals, and constructed a budget, you're in a good position to figure out how you can spend less and save more. There's a good chance that you can save money without dramatically changing your lifestyle. No matter what your situation is, there's a good chance you can reduce your spending on necessities. More than likely, you can reduce your discretionary spending without feeling deprived. Read on for simple ways to save.

UTILITIES

Utilities—electricity, gas, and water—may be necessities, but that doesn't mean that you should spend more than is absolutely necessary. Just a few minor changes in habits can result in significant savings, without any noticeable sacrifice in your lifestyle.

Unplug Your Power Adapters

Power adapters have become so common that we often don't even notice them. They plug into the wall outlets and charge the batteries on cell phones, portable computers, and MP3 players. They're necessary for the proper functioning of many hair dryers, computer monitors, and all sorts of other electronic devices. What these adapters do is "step down" 110-volt current to a much lower voltage. In the process, these devices convert electricity to heat, and they do this whether or not they're attached to whatever appliance they came with. Try this: Plug your cell phone's charger into a wall outlet, but don't connect it to your cell phone. After a few minutes, place a finger on the charger—it will feel warm to the touch. It's busy using electricity that you're paying for and shedding it as heat.

Keep Your Water Cool

Your water heater is one of the most energy-hungry appliances around. In general, there's no need to heat water to the point that it's scalding hot when it comes out of the tap. Heating water to that point is both wasteful and dangerous. You can also save on hot water by separating your colored clothes from the white ones and washing the colored clothes in cold water or warm water. Not only will you save on your gas or electric bill but your colored clothes will look better longer. And when you do need to wash something in hot water, use the appropriate setting for the size of your load. There's no point in filling the machine to the very top with hot water to wash just a few small items.

Update Your Fridge

Your refrigerator is another major energy consumer. To decrease its appetite for power, make sure the condenser coils at the back of your refrigerator are clean. Your refrigerator will work more efficiently if you take the trouble to pull it away from the wall every few months and vacuum the dust and dirt that gathers on the coils. Depending on how old your refrigerator is, you might also consider replacing it. If your refrigerator was manufactured before 2001, it may use almost 3 times the electricity that an older model uses.

See Things in a New Light

The type of incandescent bulb that has been available for more than a century is extremely inefficient in converting electricity to light. If you were to touch an incandescent bulb you'd burn your finger! You'd also quickly see that these bulbs give off as much heat as light. Fluorescent bulbs give just as much light as incandescent ones and use less than half as much electricity. Although fluorescent bulbs cost more to buy than incandescent ones, they last far longer.

Weather the Weather

Few of us can get through the winter without turning up the thermostat at least a few degrees. But there are ways to keep warm without enriching the local utility company or fuel oil dealer. One way to do that is to make certain your home is properly insulated and the windows and doors have weather stripping. If you rent your home or apartment and find that it seems drafty or that the rooms get cold quickly, it might be a good idea to ask your landlord to take action to correct the problem. No matter what your living situation, there are ways to save on heating. Putting on a sweater will cost you far less than turning up your thermostat. And during daylight hours, you can open curtains to take advantage of solar heating.

Of course, the same principles, applied in reverse, hold true in warm weather. Good insulation and appropriate clothing will reduce the need to run your air conditioner. And drawing the curtains will keep the sun from heating your home's interior.

Turn It Off

Make turning off lights and appliances a habit. When you leave a room, turn the lights off. When you are not watching it, turn the television off. When you take a break from using your computer, turn it off—or at least adjust the settings so that the monitor shuts down if the computer isn't used for an hour.

Close the Tap

Water is something we can't do without, but that doesn't mean it has to be a budget-breaker. Simple steps like shutting off the tap while brushing your teeth can save many gallons. Repairing toilets that don't shut off as soon as the tank refills and faucets that drip can also save water. Most lawns need to be watered only 5 minutes every other day; flower beds similarly need to be watered for only a short time, particularly if you use drip irrigation.

FOOD

As with utilities, food is a necessity that offers plenty of opportunities to cut spending. There's no need to eat less; with a few simple changes to your routine, you can save on your food bill.

Make a List and Stick to It

Grocery stores offer virtually endless opportunities to waste money on impulse purchases, but it is possible to avoid those unnecessary expenditures. The key is good planning. If you plan what you're going to cook over the next few days and then make a list of the items you need to buy, you're less likely to buy unnecessary items that will either spoil before you can use them or sit in the pantry. Sticking to the list takes discipline, but doing so is worth the effort. Not only do you avoid unnecessary impulse purchases but you waste time and gasoline returning to the store to buy the one or two vital ingredients you forgot on the first trip. Finally, experts say that impulse buying can be avoided by not shopping hungry. It's all too easy to waste money on snack foods or expensive pre-processed foods if you go into the store with your stomach growling from hunger.

Cut Out Coupons

Although the advertisements that come in the mail can seem like an annoying waste of paper, it's worth scanning these circulars for discount coupons. In addition, some retailers have begun offering coupons that can be downloaded from the Internet and printed out. Coupons can be stored in a file and then pulled out when you've finished making your shopping list. Although it is probably a waste of money to make a lengthy detour to buy a single item on sale, it's often possible to plan a shopping trip so that you can take advantage of sales at two different grocery stores.

Join the Club

Most major grocery chains feature some sort of club program that affords discounts to members. The customer provides a name, address, and phone number and is then given a membership card. To take advantage of member discounts, the customer simply gives the card to the cashier or punches in his or her telephone number on a keypad. Stores hope to build customer loyalty with these club programs and, as with coupon offers, to sell other items at full price once the customer is in the store. However, by choosing purchases carefully and sticking to your list, you can save on your grocery bill.

Keep Shelf Life in Mind

When it comes to perishable items, such as produce and dairy products, buying only what you can easily consume will save you lots of money. Supermarkets frequently offer 2-for-1 sales, or offer a reduced price on a second, identical item. For example, many grocery stores charge $4 for a gallon of milk, but charge $6 for two gallons. But those savings disappear (and then some!) if the second gallon spoils before you can use it. When purchasing canned and dry goods, however, the opposite holds true. When items you regularly use come on sale, there's nothing wrong with stocking up. Items like dried pasta will last for months if they're properly stored, and canned soups and vegetables will keep for years.

Put On Your Chef's Hat

There's no doubt that cooking for yourself is cheaper than eating in a restaurant, since you're only paying for ingredients and a little electricity or gas. Better yet, many people find that cooking is an excellent creative outlet. Cooking for yourself is generally healthier than eating in restaurants, since it allows you to control the size of portions, the ingredients you use, and the cooking method.

Cooking can be a bit daunting at first, since cookbooks use terminology that can be unfamiliar, and the recipes can be complex. But with just a little practice, it becomes easy to assemble even complicated dishes without getting stressed out. If you find the idea of cooking intimidating, someone at your local bookstore can probably steer you to a good cookbook aimed at beginners. There are websites on the Internet that offer easy recipes as well.

Brown-bag It

Depending on where you work, you may or may not have extensive options of where you eat lunch. What is almost certain, though, is that a lunch purchased at even the most modest restaurant is likely to cost you $10, and maybe more. That works out to $50 per week. Even if you assume that you only work 48 weeks a year, that adds up to at least $2400. Think of what you can buy with that kind of money! You can save yourself expensive lunchtime trips by taking a few minutes to make yourself a sandwich or pack some leftovers to take to work with you. As is true with your home-cooked dinners, the lunch you make for yourself is guaranteed to be prepared just the way you like it!

FUEL

There's no avoiding buying fuel (cars have to eat, too!) Though there is little to be done about escalating gas prices, there are a few basic ways that will help you reduce how much you spend at the pump.

Give That Car a Checkup

A good time to have your car's systems checked is when you have the oil changed. At the same time they change the oil, most technicians routinely check your car's air filter. If the filter is dirty, replacing it can improve your car's fuel economy. In any case, having your car's oil changed according to the manufacturer's recommendations will lengthen the engine's life and keep it running smoothly.

Check Your Tires

The less air a tire has in it, the more it resists rolling, so if your tires are under-inflated, your engine will have to work harder—and use more fuel. Of course, under-inflated tires are also likely to wear out sooner than ones that are kept at the right pressure. The same technician who changes your engine oil will most likely also check your tires' pressure and add air if necessary.

Your Car Should Lose a Few Pounds

The heavier the car, the harder its engine has to work and the more fuel it will use. To maximize fuel economy, avoid hauling heavy items like tools and books around unless you need to. The one exception to this rule, of course, is passengers in a carpool. Depending on what kind of agreement you make with your fellow carpoolers, you'll either save on fuel by sharing the driving responsibilities, or get some help from your passengers in purchasing fuel.

Keep on Rolling

Avoid letting your engine idle. Modern automobile engines are designed to be put to work as soon as you start them, so there is no need for them to warm up. The kind of stop-and-go driving that occurs on crowded freeways wastes fuel as well, so it makes sense to avoid rush-hour driving if you can. If you can, run errands at off-times, such as on weekends. Finally, even if traffic isn't heavy, avoid the temptation to accelerate fast or drive at high speeds. Not only will you save fuel, but you'll arrive safely at your destination.

Don't Wait to Fill Up

It may be gratifying to find a station selling gas cheap at just the moment when the needle on your gas gauge is hitting the "E" mark. Aside from the obvious danger of finding yourself out of gas miles from any station, running on empty can be bad for your engine. Over time, most cars collect sediment in their gas tank; when you run your car until it's empty, you risk sucking some of that sediment into your engine's carburetor. The result can be reduced engine performance or stalling. And if the fuel filter becomes completely clogged, your engine could stop running altogether. You can buy several tanks of gas with the money you'd spend paying a mechanic to change your fuel filter. It's also worth keeping in mind that gas prices tend to go up and down depending on the day of the week. Experts say that gas prices are lowest on Tuesday and Wednesday. With a little planning, you can take advantage of lower fuel prices.

Plan Your Day

If you have many stops to make in one day, organize your route so you minimize the distance you drive. Less distance means less gas consumed.

CLOTHING

Get Double-duty From Your Clothes

You'll get the most of your clothing budget if you focus on garments that can serve multiple purposes or be used for years. For example, a well-made, conservatively styled suit is unlikely to go out of fashion and can be worn for many years. Experts also say that when it comes to clothing, cheaper is not necessarily better. Although it may be tempting to buy a garment for $9.99, it's very likely that a garment that sells for $29.99 will turn out to be the better deal because it lasts longer.

Buy What You Can Wear—Now

It is always tempting to buy clothes based on the size we want to be rather than the size we are. Men and women both sometimes make the mistake of buying clothes that are too small in hopes that it will motivate them to lose weight or get in shape. However, swallowing your pride and buying clothes that fit properly will do more for your appearance (and self-esteem) than having a closet full of garments that turned out to be a waste of money.

Buy Clothes in the Off-Season

Buying clothing in the off-season can result in significant savings. Most retailers have limited space, and so they'll discount garments heavily to make room for more seasonal items. Particularly for items like winter coats or boots, which are less susceptible to fashion trends, it makes sense to buy when the price is lower rather than when you need them the most.

Watch for Sales

A related technique for saving money on clothes is to take advantage of the retailers' need to move their merchandise. Retailers want to generate revenue (that is, sales) and will often offer significant discounts to do so. As a result, major retail chains start putting merchandise on sale weeks before a major holiday, like Christmas. That said, you will also find a lot of quality clothes in the days immediately after the Christmas shopping season. The key to saving money on clothing is patience. With luck, you will be rewarded with a great find that is marked down as much as 75 percent from its original price.

Be Gentle with Your Clothes

Make sure you follow the manufacturer's guidelines for proper care of your clothes (which can be found on their tags). Proper cleaning will preserve their size, shape, and color for a long time. It may be tempting to avoid spending $10 on dry cleaning, but washing a $60 blouse and having it shrink or discolor is not a cost-effective choice. The least expensive option, of course, is to buy a washable garment in the first place. But even if your clothes are washable, it's often desirable—and appropriate—to get more than one day's wear between launderings. Cotton slacks, for example, can be worn many times before they need to be washed.

ENTERTAINMENT

Spending money on entertainment is hardly a "must." This is a spending category in which you can make deep cuts. It's also possible to reduce spending on entertainment without radically cramping your lifestyle.

Buy Movie Tickets at the Theater

Many major theater chains offer the option of buying tickets online. Unfortunately, they often charge extra for this service. Buying online assures that you'll get a seat at a popular film and allows you to avoid standing in a long line outside the theater, but you'll pay a dollar or two for this convenience. Some discount retailers sell books of passes that can be used at specified theater. Of course, it's a good idea to call the theater you're planning to attend ahead of time to make certain that the passes you've purchased will be accepted.

See A Matinee

Tickets always cost less during the day than they do during the evening. If your schedule permits, you can save two or three dollars per ticket. As a bonus, the theaters won't be as crowded in the middle of the day.

Avoid the Snack Bar

Movie theaters and sporting event venues charge a premium for the items they sell at the snack bar. You may not have much choice but to pay the inflated prices. However, many theaters object if patrons come in carrying ice cream cones or bags of popcorn. If you want to bring your own snacks, stop at convenience store ahead of time and be discrete—small items such as candy bars or mints are unlikely to cause a problem with the management.

Look for Discounted Tickets

Most public attractions—major theme parks, museums, and zoos—offer discounts of 10 to 15 percent to members of organizations like the Auto Club, various labor unions, and the military. In addition, retired people and students usually qualify for discounts. Because museums and zoos consider education to be a major part of their function, teachers are often given substantial discounts.

Keep Up with All the Special Deals

Many public attractions periodically offer discounts of as much as 50 percent on memberships or year-long passes as a way of bringing in new customers. Such offers usually are meant to increase traffic when demand is slow. Sometimes, a major theme park will allow a customer who buys a single day's admission to exchange that ticket for a year-long pass with no additional charge. For families who live within easy driving distance of such an attraction, this can amount to savings of hundreds of dollars over the course of a year.

Community Events

Most urban areas offer local events, such as street fairs, open-air concerts, or seasonal celebrations like Oktoberfest or Mardi Gras. Local high schools put on plays and concerts, and members of the general public are generally welcome to attend. Similarly, community colleges and universities almost always have some kind of performance going on. Admission to such performances is often just a few dollars per person. Not only do you get inexpensive entertainment, but the students gain valuable experience performing in front of an audience.

PHONE

Telephones are such a part of our lives that spending money for them is hardly optional. That said, your telephone service offers many opportunities for cutting expenses.

Monitor Your Usage

Telecommunications companies aggressively market themselves, offering service in a large array of packages. You can often find a company that will give you discounts in return for allowing them to provide all your telecommunications services. You may find that a single company can provide not only your telephone but also Internet connection and even cable television service. In addition to qualifying you for discounts, working with a single company offers the added advantage of having just one bill to keep track of. Keep in mind, though, that package deals constantly change, so it's a good idea to periodically call the company to make certain you're getting all the discounts you qualify for. At the same time, you may decide that you're not really using extra services you're paying for, such as call waiting or caller I.D.

Pay in Advance

Although it's possible to direct-dial a long distance call, that's not necessarily the cheapest alternative. Large discount stores sell telephone calling cards that allow you to call virtually anywhere in the world for a fraction of the cost of a direct-dialed call. Cards of this sort are particularly useful when you're traveling, since hotels often charge exorbitant surcharges when guests make calls from their room.

Dial on Nights and Weekends

Telephone companies typically charge less for long distance calls during "off" hours. Calls made on weekends tend to cost less than calls made on weekdays, for example. Depending on where you live, you can reach someone who lives in a different time zone and get a discounted rate without having to call in the middle of the night.

CAR

Only in a handful of American cities is it practical (or even possible) to do without a car. However, with a little research and careful thought you can save thousands of dollars on the cost of buying, driving, and maintaining a car.

Buying A Car: Know What You Want

Nothing is likely to set your head spinning faster than a visit to a car dealer, and that's particularly true if you walk in without some ideas on what your needs are. Car dealers, naturally, want to make money on the sale of a vehicle, and their sales people are trained to sell you as much car as they can. If all you need is a small car that will get you to work and back home again, you may still end up with a six-passenger, all-wheel-drive SUV unless you keep your requirements firmly in mind. If you're buying a new car, you should think in advance about some of the optional equipment you want. Car dealers make a lot of money on things like moon roofs, a 6-CD changer, and navigation systems; be prepared to say "no" many times as your sales person tries to persuade you to pile on the options.

Watch for Add-ons

Imagine that you've negotiated a satisfactory price for the car you want and need. Before you're handed the keys, you'll probably be steered into the office of someone with a title like "assistant sales manager." That individual's job is to sell you all kinds of extras that you may neither need nor want. This person will likely discuss things like protective coatings on the car's exterior, optional theft-protection devices, and extended warranties. Such add-ons cost the dealer next to nothing, but they can end up costing you thousands of dollars.

Leasing Versus Buying

If you lack the cash for a down payment on a car, you may be able to benefit from leasing. You'll still need to come up with some cash, but it's usually a smaller amount than you would need to purchase a car. The drawback to leasing, of course, is that you pay hundreds of dollars every month, but at the end of the term of the lease—usually several years—you don't own the car. By contrast, if you buy a car, once you've paid off the loan, the car is yours; if you chose well and take care of it, that car may continue to serve you for years to come. The other factor you must consider in deciding between leasing and buying is how much you expect to drive the car. Leases usually include a clause that imposes significant charges if you drive the car more than a specified number of miles before the lease is up. These charges can cost you hundreds, or even thousands, of dollars—and you still won't have a car to call your own at the end of the lease.

Change Your Car's Oil

Nothing can ensure the longevity and efficiency of your engine more than changing the oil at the intervals the manufacturer recommends. Changing the oil regularly reduces the likelihood of your car needing expensive repairs. It's a good idea to keep a clear record of oil changes. If you do encounter a major problem, you may need to prove that your engine was properly maintained in order to have it fixed under the terms of the warranty.

Balance Your Tires

As tires wear, they eventually get out of balance. The result is a rougher, noisier ride. If tires are allowed to stay out of balance for a long time, the car's shock absorbers wear out faster, and replacing those is far more expensive than the few dollars that tire-balancing costs. Another consideration is that if you ever have a problem with the tires, you may need to prove that you had the tires balanced regularly in order for them to be covered under their manufacturer's warranty.

Insurance: Rewards for Reducing Risk

Automobile insurance is not an optional purchase, but there are still plenty of ways you can reduce your insurance costs. Insurance companies use all kinds of statistics to calculate the chances that they'll have to pay out money if you have an accident or if your car is stolen. The more ways you can reduce those chances, the lower your insurance costs will be. For example, many insurance companies offer discounts if a car is equipped with a burglar alarm. If you or someone who will be driving your car is a student, there's a good chance that the insurance company will offer reduced rates if the young driver can prove that he or she consistently earns A's and B's in school. (Statistically, good students have fewer accidents than poor students.) Finally, your insurance premiums are typically based on how many miles you drive a day (the logic being that the more time you spend on the road, the more likely you are to have an accident). If a job change results in reduced commuting distance, reporting this to your insurance company can save you hundreds of dollars on your premiums.

RENT

If you have not yet managed to save enough money for a down payment, or if buying a home right now isn't appropriate, you still have opportunities to save money on rent or to make renting work to your advantage.

Lease-Purchase Option

Perhaps you have the resources to buy a home but feel the time might not be right. Waiting to purchase a home makes sense if you're just starting a new job and aren't sure whether it's secure enough to justify committing yourself to making mortgage payments. Depending on economic conditions in your community, you might be able to negotiate a lease-purchase option. The way this works is that you negotiate a purchase price with the seller just as if you're buying the home. But instead of going on to get a mortgage, you agree with the seller to rent the property for a period of time—usually a year. At the end of the year, you can either go through with the purchase or you can walk away. If you go through with the purchase, part of the rent you paid over the previous year could go towards the purchase price of the home.

Rent Reduction: It Pays To Be a Good Tenant

If you're renting, it's unlikely that you can cut expenses by negotiating an outright reduction of your rent. You can, however, take steps to keep any increases in rent to a minimum. The key to keeping your rent down is to be a good tenant. Above all else, that means making your rent payments on time. Trustworthy tenants can be hard to find; if you've paid on time, your landlord will be less likely to raise your rent when it is time to renew or extend your lease. Most landlords would prefer to stick with a tenant they know rather than search for a new renter whose dependability is an unknown.

Some landlords will allow a tenant to do work around the property in exchange for a reduction in rent. A tenant who is handy with tools might be able to trade maintenance services for rent. For example, you can offer to paint the house or mow the lawn in return for a reduced monthly rent.

HOME IMPROVEMENT AND MAINTENANCE

Get Estimates in Writing

Unless you're living in a newly built house, it's likely you'll want to have work done on your home eventually. If you're like most people, you'll have to hire a contractor to do at least some of the work. When it comes time to hire a contractor, be certain to get clear estimates that specify what work will be done and for how much money. Hiring someone who makes vague verbal offers to work cheap is very likely to result in a job that is half-done—if it gets done at all. Even if a contractor provides a detailed written estimate, it's not a good idea to pay for all the work in advance. Most reputable contractors split the total fee into three equal payments. Usually, they ask for the first payment up front before any work is begun. The second payment generally is not required until the project reaches an agreed-upon point. For example, if the kitchen is being remodeled, the second payment might be due just before the countertops are installed. The final payment should not be made until the entire project is finished to your satisfaction.

Do-It-Yourself

If you have a project that you know you can handle, you can save money by not hiring a contractor. Of course, only you can know if you have the time to take on the job. You also have to be prepared to discover, once you've begun work, that there was more to the project than you realized. If that happens, you may have fewer options in hiring help—especially if you've made the house unlivable in the process of starting the project! You might be able to save yourself some headaches in this regard by hiring someone who's willing to coach you while you do most of the work and who will intervene in case of an emergency.

For most people, do-it-yourself projects are more likely to be satisfying (and successful) if they're confined to the outdoors. If you have a yard, you can avoid paying gardeners or landscapers and still be pleased with the results. A few hundred dollars worth of tools and a lawnmower can quickly pay for themselves. Not only will doing your own yard work save you money but gardening can be an effective stress-reducer. If you occasionally find there are tasks that are too much for you, or if you simply need an extra pair of strong arms, you might well find a neighborhood teenager who will help out for a modest amount.

Keeping expenses down—and actively looking for ways to cut spending—makes good financial sense. It stands to reason that whatever you don't spend can be saved. The less money you spend unnecessarily, the more you'll have available to help you meet your financial goals.

UNDERSTANDING INTEREST RATES

Although the term "interest rate" is a familiar one, very few know how interest rates actually work. Almost daily, the news media reports that the Federal Reserve Bank (FED) is raising or lowering rates, but few people understand what this means. Learning about interest rates is to your advantage; this knowledge will help you save money, make wise financial decisions, and ultimately become wealthy.

Interest is what lenders charge borrowers for the use of their money. That charge is calculated as a percentage of the amount that was loaned—what's known as principal. Lenders make their profits through the interest they charge borrowers. Whenever you borrow money from a financial institution such as a bank, credit union, mortgage company, or credit card company, the loan will be charged interest.

These types of interest rates are commonly referred to as a loan's annual percentage rate (APR). Simply put, an APR is the overall "cost" of a loan. That means it includes any up-front fees the lender charges and any advance interest, known as "points." For example, if you purchase a car and get a loan for 8 percent, the APR will actually be somewhat greater than 8 percent, a reflection of the various fees the lender tacked on to the loan. Because fees can vary widely from one lender to the next, including those in the calculation of the APR makes comparing the loans they offer much more accurate.

INTEREST RATES AND FINANCE CHARGES IN PLAIN ENGLISH

Let's say you want to purchase an $18,000 car and you want to pay for it in monthly installments over 5 years. If you were offered a zero percent interest rate, your monthly payments would be $300 for the duration of the term.

Unfortunately, those who make car loans are not usually that generous. They may occasionally offer very low promotional rates for those with exceptionally good credit. But more commonly, automobile buyers will be charged anywhere from 1 to 10 percent on the loan.

The interest charged by a lender can add considerably to the cost of a purchase. Returning to the example of the $18,000 car above, let's pretend that the salesperson offered to finance the entire amount of the car at an interest rate of 7 percent. This would make your monthly car payment $356.42. Since this is a 5-year loan, you'll write 60 checks, each one for $356.42. If you do the math, you'll find that the car you thought you were buying for $18,000 actually cost you $21,385.29.

UNDERSTANDING INTEREST RATES

Home mortgages work much the same way as car loans. The amount you pay each month is determined by the amount you're borrowing, the interest rate, and the term—that is, the time you have to pay it off. The loan amounts are far larger and the term of the mortgage is longer. A term of 30 years is common in home mortgages.

MORTGAGE PAYMENT CALCULATOR

The following table will help you determine your mortgage payment based on the loan amount. Follow the simple steps to calculate your monthly payments.

STEP 1: Take the amount of money you would like to borrow and divide it by 1,000.

STEP 2: Follow the row corresponding to the interest rate your lender is currently offering to the 15-year mortgage or the 30-year mortgage column, depending on which you plan to apply for, and find the appropriate number, which is known as the multiplication factor.

STEP 3: Multiply the number you got in Step 1 by the number you got in Step 2. The resulting figure will be your mortgage payment. For example, if you want a loan amount of $400,000, start by dividing that by 1,000. This will give you 400. Now, let's say that your bank is offering you a 30-year loan at a 6.5 percent fixed rate. The multiplication factor under the 30-year mortgage column for the 6.5 percent interest rate is 6.33. Now multiply 400 by 6.33 and you will get that your monthly mortgage payment will be $2,532. This would be your Principal + Interest, or PI.

Mortgage Calculator
To use this table simply multiply a number in either the 15-year or 30-year mortgage against the size of your mortgage.

PERCENTAGE OF INTEREST RATE	MULTIPLICATION FACTOR FOR 15- YEAR MORTGAGE	MULTIPLICATION FACTOR FOR 30-YEAR MORTGAGE
4	7.40	4.77
4.5	7.65	5.07
5	7.91	5.37
5.5	8.18	5.68
6	8.44	6.00
6.5	8.72	6.33
7	8.99	6.65
7.5	9.28	7.00

PERCENTAGE OF INTEREST RATE	MULTIPLICATION FACTOR FOR 15- YEAR MORTGAGE	MULTIPLICATION FACTOR FOR 30-YEAR MORTGAGE
8	9.56	7.34
8.5	9.85	7.69
9	10.15	8.05
9.5	10.45	8.41
10	10.75	8.78
10.5	11.06	9.15
11	11.37	9.53
11.5	11.69	9.91
12	12.01	10.29
12.5	12.17	10.4

The monthly payments on a fixed-rate mortgage are always the same. What changes is the amount of principal and interest paid in each payment. During the early years in the life of your loan, most of your monthly payment goes toward paying interest and very little goes toward paying off the actual loan. But as you make payments over the years, more money goes toward paying off your loan; since the amount owed is reduced, the interest charged is reduced. To illustrate this, we have laid out a table showing the amount of principal and interest that are paid in the first 12 months and in the last 12 months for the following loan:

- Amount of the loan: $100,000
- Payments per year: 12
- Duration of the loan: 30 years
- Annual interest rate: 7%

According to the mortgage calculator above, your monthly payment would be $665. If you look at the table on the next page, you can see the amount of money that is actually applied toward principal and interest in your $665.30 payment for the first and last 12 months. It is interesting to note that in your first payment, only $81.97 is going toward the principal and $583.33 is going toward interest. In your last payment, $661.31 is going toward the principal and only $3.86 is going toward interest.

To calculate this, you need to multiply the amount of money owed in any given month by your interest rate. In this case, when you make your first payment, you owe $100,000 at the 7 percent interest rate; therefore, you would multiply $100,000 x .07 and divide this number by 12 months. This will give you $583.33, or the amount of money that you pay in interest during the first month of that loan. To find the amount of money that goes toward the principal of your loan, you need to subtract the amount of money that went toward the interest from your monthly payment. $665.30 - $583.33 = $81.97.

Now, for the next month, the actual amount owed is $100,000 minus $81.97 or $99,918.03. Since you owe less money in the second month, less of your payment will go toward the interest and more toward the principal. This continues each month until the end of the 30-year term. You start paying more money toward your principal and less money toward interest after 21.1 years or 253 payments.

It is also interesting to note the amount of money in interest that you will pay in 30 years. In this example, you end up paying $139,508.75 in interest for your $100,000 loan. That's why it is recommended that you pay your loan off as fast as you can by making a few extra payments each year.

PAYMENT SCHEDULE FOR A $100,000 LOAN AT 7% INTEREST, 30-YEAR FIXED RATE MORTGAGE

MONTHLY PAYMENT	INTEREST RATE	PAYMENT AMOUNT	INTEREST PORTION	PRINCIPAL REDUCTION	MORTGAGE BALANCE
1	7	$665.30	$583.33	$81.97	$99,918.03
2	7	$665.30	$582.86	$82.45	$99,835.59
3	7	$665.30	$582.37	$82.93	$99,752.66
4	7	$665.30	$581.89	$83.41	$99,669.24
5	7	$665.30	$581.40	$81.97	$99,585.34
6	7	$665.30	$580.91	$82.45	$99,500.95
7	7	$665.30	$580.42	$82.93	$99,416.07
8	7	$665.30	$579.93	$83.41	$99,330.70
9	7	$665.30	$579.43	$83.90	$99,244.82
10	7	$665.30	$578.93	$84.39	$99,158.45
11	7	$665.30	$578.42	$84.88	$99,071.57
12	7	$665.30	$577.92	$85.38	$98,984.19
349	7	$665.30	$44.85	$85.87	$7,068.40
350	7	$665.30	$41.23	$86.37	$6,444.33
351	7	$665.30	$37.59	$86.88	$5,816.62
352	7	$665.30	$33.93	$87.39	$5,185.25
353	7	$665.30	$30.25	$620.45	$4,550.19
354	7	$665.30	$26.54	$624.07	$3,911.43
355	7	$665.30	$22.82	$627.71	$3,268.95
356	7	$665.30	$19.07	$631.37	$2,622.71
357	7	$665.30	$15.30	$635.06	$1,972.71
358	7	$665.30	$11.51	$638.76	$1,318.92
359	7	$665.30	$7.69	$642.49	$661.31
360	7	$665.30	$3.86	$646.23	$0.00

What all of this means, of course, is that the interest rate paid on a loan greatly increases the cost of purchasing a home. If income and other expenses allow, some homebuyers choose to take a 15-year mortgage as a way of reducing their interest expense. That $400,000 mortgage with a 6.5 percent interest rate and a 15-year term will have a monthly payment of $3,488, but the total interest paid will be far less than what would be paid on a 30-year mortgage.

Of course, you may not be able to afford a 15-year mortgage. What you can do, however, is add on to your payment each month, and the lender will apply this extra cash against the principal. Depending on how much extra you pay, the mortgage can be paid off years early, saving you many thousands of dollars in interest expense. You can also make an extra monthly payment each year. If you did this on a $400,000 mortgage with a 6.5 percent interest rate, you'd pay off your mortgage in less than 25 years instead of 30 years.

INTEREST AND SAVINGS ACCOUNTS

Just as you pay interest on a loan, banks and other financial institutions pay interest to you when you deposit money with them. Banks use the money deposited with them and lend it out to other customers at a higher interest rate than the one they pay the account holder. The difference in those percentages is one way the bank makes a profit.

Interest rates for deposits are quoted as the annual percentage yield (APY). How high an interest rate the bank offers depends on how easily you can withdraw the money. For example, you can simply walk into the bank and withdraw your money if it's in a passbook savings account, but the APY will be quite low. Lower still is the APY on checking accounts, if any interest is paid at all. Banks pay the highest APY if the customer agrees not to withdraw the money for a certain period of time. Customers usually can withdraw their money early but have to pay high fees for doing so. In deciding what kind of account to deposit your money in, it's important to consider how much access you need to have to the funds.

Once you deposit money in an account, it begins to earn interest, and the amount you have in the account grows through a process known as compounding. Compounding means that the interest the bank pays goes into the account and interest is paid on that money as well. The more frequently the interest is compounded, the more money you will earn. Daily compounding is better than weekly compounding, which is better than monthly compounding, and so on.

The following example will help you make more sense of compounding. Let's say you open a savings account with $15,000 with a 5 percent APY. If the interest were to be compounded daily, on Day 2 the bank would add $2.05 to your balance ($15,000 multiplied by 5 percent, divided by 365 days in a year). That $2.05 is added to the balance in the account. Then, on Day 3, interest is calculated again, using the new balance of $15,002.05. Therefore, on Day 3 you would earn $2.06 in interest ($15,002.05 multiplied by 5 percent, divided by 365). As you can see, the longer your money remains in the account, the more interest it will earn. (Most banks now use a complicated calculation known as continuous compounding, which allows your money to grow faster still.)

Banks frequently change the APY they offer as a way of competing for customers. Usually, though, the APY the bank pays on your particular account remains at the level agreed upon when you opened the account.

CREDIT-CARD INTEREST

Depending on the type of account you open with a bank, you might be offered a credit card as well. Make no mistake, however: Banks offer credit cards because they make a lot of money off them. No matter how much interest the bank is paying you on the money you deposit, that's literally small change compared to the interest you'll be charged if you run up a large balance on your credit card.

Some banks offer low introductory rates—perhaps 6 or 7 percent—on the balance a customer owes on a credit card, but that rate remains in effect only for a limited time (typically six months). After this period, rates often skyrocket. Rates of 15 percent and higher are quite common.

Paying such high interest rates can make it very difficult for someone to get out of debt, but that's just fine as far as banks are concerned. Part of every credit-card agreement is a requirement that the cardholder make a minimum payment on the balance every month. This minimum payment can seem very modest, but what credit-card issuers don't make clear is that most of the money goes toward paying interest. For example, it's quite common for people to be carrying a balance of $5,000; it's also quite common for banks to set the minimum payment on that balance at $125. Unfortunately for the cardholder who makes only minimum payments, it will take over 26 years to pay off that balance!

Banks make a lot of money off credit cards, and because of this they try to motivate their customers to make purchases using the cards. Some banks, for example, offer a cash rebate on purchases made with their cards. Of course, unless you pay off your balance every month, the cash rebate is quickly eaten up by the credit-card interest. Another popular incentive is a free airplane ticket once you've charged a certain amount—say, $25,000—on the card. Again, because of the high interest rates credit-card balances carry, a "free" airplane ticket can end up costing you more than a luxury cruise. As we noted in Chapter 2, credit-card interest can turn out to be enormously expensive, which is why paying off your credit-card balance should be one of your main short-term goals.

SAVINGS

Securing your financial future requires that you start saving money—the sooner, the better. You have many choices of where to put your savings. As we've already discussed, banks and credit unions offer savings accounts, which can be opened with as little as $25. Stock brokerage companies also offer various savings options, although the minimum deposit the large brokerage firms will accept may be higher than what banks accept. If you're just starting to put aside savings, a bank or credit union probably makes the most sense.

BANKS

When you deposit money in a bank account, you may have some options. Banks commonly offer savings accounts, which are a safe and stable choice. As we discussed in Chapter 5, savings accounts are wise if you anticipate that you may need quick access to your money at some point. You will not be charged a penalty for withdrawing money (although the bank may charge you a monthly fee if the balance drops below a certain amount). Savings accounts are very safe, too, since the federal government, through an agency known as the Federal Deposit Insurance Corporation (FDIC), insures such accounts up to $100,000. This means that if the bank was ever to fail (a rare event, but one that does happen from time to time), the federal government will make sure the depositors get their money back.

SAVINGS ACCOUNT OPTIONS

There are two primary types of savings accounts: passbook savings and statement savings. With passbook accounts, deposits and withdrawals are recorded in a small paper book that the bank gives you when you open the account. Passbooks are typically used for accounts that have a low number of transactions. Because the account's balance is physically written in the book by a teller every time a deposit or a withdrawal is made, the account holder can always tell how much money he or she has. Today, this type of savings account has become less common, in favor of accounts that allow customers to access their account history either via their bank's website or at an automated teller machine (ATM).

Statement savings accounts are similar to passbook accounts, except that instead of manually recording your account activity in a passbook, the bank will send you a monthly statement that indicates all your account activity—for example, deposits, withdrawals, and interest credits. This information is now almost always available online as well. Both passbook and statement savings accounts may require a minimum balance in order to earn interest. In addition, some institutions require a minimum balance for these accounts (typically ranging between $100 and $250). If you fall below the minimum balance, an account maintenance fee may be imposed, which will be charged every month your balance falls short of the requirement.

Every bank offers savings accounts, so you have many choices when you decide to open one. As we've already seen, banks try to gain customers by offering more attractive interest rates than competing banks. This means in deciding on a bank to use, you can shop around in order to get the best interest rate. Sometimes, it pays to talk to a bank's manager to gain a better interest rate than the advertised one.

In deciding on a bank, people often consider convenience. Many large banks have hundreds of branch offices. Often, you can find a small branch located in a supermarket or large discount department store. Sometimes, though, a smaller bank with fewer branches offers higher interest rates. Since almost all banks, regardless of size, offer customers the ability to access their account information online, you may decide it doesn't matter whether your bank is just up the street or not. Depending on the bank, you may even be able to transfer funds into and out of your account electronically. In fact, there are also a number of Internet banks that do all of their business online. Because Internet banks do not have to maintain physical branches, their expenses are relatively low. As a result, they generally pay higher interest rates than more traditional "brick and mortar" banks. In exchange for not being able to talk directly to a live teller, you may be able to earn an APR of over 5 percent.

One thing to be cautious of is that a bank that pays a high interest rate on savings may also charge higher fees than other banks do. Before opening an account, you should ask the bank for a copy of its fee disclosure statement, which will outline all fees and restrictions imposed on an account. As we've noted, some banks will charge a fee if your balance drops below a certain minimum. Others may charge a maintenance fee if the account does not have any activity over a period of time. Also keep in mind that if you withdraw money via an ATM, there may be fees imposed if you use a machine that is not owned by your bank. The bank that owns the ATM may charge you up to $2 per transaction, and your own bank may also charge you for using a machine out of their network. By making certain that you understand all the fees and restrictions associated with your account, you can avoid being hit with surprise charges.

No matter where you open your savings account, be aware that the FDIC only insures deposits up to a total of $100,000 per customer, per bank. If you happen to have more than $100,000 to deposit, you'll need to break it up and open accounts in more than one bank.

CERTIFICATE OF DEPOSIT (CD)

Most banks offer certificates of deposit. In return for getting a higher APY than savings accounts offer, you promise not to withdraw your money for a specified period of time—for example, 3, 6, or 9 months.

Much like savings accounts, CDs are insured by the FDIC and are therefore risk-free. CDs are a good choice if you do not need immediate access to your money. Although you can cash out or "liquidate" a CD at any time, if you do so prior to the end of its term (also known as the CD's "maturity date"), you will incur a financial penalty.

The maturity date of a CD is important for another reason. Typically, money invested for longer periods of time will earn the best APY, so the further off the maturity date is, the more interest you'll earn. Three-month CDs will have the lowest APY, while 5-year CDs will offer the highest APY. However, because of the fees that are charged for early withdrawals, it's important to think carefully about whether you might need access to your money before the CD matures. It might be tempting to invest in a long-term CD to get the higher APY. But, that higher return on your investment may be eaten up by fees if you liquidate the CD prior to its maturity date. It's worth asking about fees for early liquidation, though, since banks sometimes compete by offering long-term CDs with very low penalties for cashing out early.

CDs vary depending on their terms and APY. In addition, they vary according to other features. Although these variations can be confusing, there are basically six types of CDs:

Traditional CD
These are the most common and popular types of CDs and may also be referred to as "fixed rate" CDs. You invest your money for a specified amount of time at a fixed interest rate. Once that time is up, you have the option of either cashing out the CD or "rolling it over," which amounts to reinvesting your money for another specified period of time). One interesting feature of traditional CDs is that banks typically allow you to add to the principal balance of the CD during the course of the term. This is helpful if you unexpectedly find yourself with additional cash.

Bump-Up CD
Whereas the APY of traditional CDs doesn't change, Bump-Up CDs allow you the option to raise, or "bump up," your APY if interest rates rise. In return for this flexibility, bump-up CDs typically pay a lower APY than traditional CDs do. This means that if interest rates do not rise significantly, you will earn less interest than you would have had you locked into a traditional CD. Banks that offer bump-up CDs typically limit how many times a customer can bump up the interest rate. While many banks only allow their customers to take advantage of this option once during the course of the term, there are others that allow for two and even three bumps.

Liquid CD
A liquid CD allows the customer to withdraw money from the CD without paying a penalty for doing so. The cost of this greater liquidity is a lower APY than a traditional CD of the same term would offer. Liquid CDs are sometimes referred to as Fee-Free or No Penalty CDs.

The terms and conditions of liquid CDs vary widely from bank to bank and need to be looked at carefully. With some banks, for example, a withdrawal will mean termination of the account. Others allow you to make withdrawals so long as a minimum balance is maintained. Sometimes, the interest rate on the CD drops if the customer withdraws more than a specified amount. The federal government requires that owners of liquid CDs wait at least seven days before making any withdrawal, but banks are free to set longer minimum waiting periods.

Zero-Coupon CD

Also called a "discount CD," this type of CD does not pay interest in the traditional sense. Instead, the buyer purchases the CD at a deep discount off the face value. When the CD matures, the buyer gets the full face value. These CDs typically take 15 to 20 years to reach maturity, so they are not suitable for depositors who expect to need their money within a few months or even a few years.

Callable CD

This type of CD is similar to a traditional one, except the bank has the right to pay the CD off before the agreed-upon term ends, a practice known as calling. When and if the CD is "called," the principal is returned along with all the interest accrued prior to the call date. Banks offer callable CDs when they think interest rates are likely to drop. Essentially, the bank is protecting itself from being locked into paying interest rates that are unprofitable. Usually, such CDs feature a call-protection period, during which the bank cannot call the CD even if it wants to. Callable CDs generally offer a higher interest rate than other CDs. In return for this higher rate, the customer loses some assurance regarding how much interest his or her money will earn.

Brokered CD

Brokered CDs are the same as bank CDs except they are sold by middlemen, called brokers. These CDs may pay up to 1 percent more than CDs sold by a bank. This happens because the brokers are often able to negotiate higher rates of interest by promising to buy a certain number of CDs. In exchange for getting the higher APY, you may pay the broker a modest charge for placing the order (or there may be a flat fee for each thousand dollars invested). Although you still have a safety net in that brokered CDs are insured by the FDIC, deposit brokers are not required to go through any licensing procedures. This means that there is no way of knowing how competent or honest the broker is.

The wide range of choices in CDs can work to your advantage. For example, if you don't want to lock all your money up for a period of time, you can use a strategy known as laddering your CDs. Laddering means buying CDs of varying types and terms. Laddering gives you ready access to at least some of your cash while allowing you to earn the maximum interest from the bulk of your money. For example, if you have $3,000 you'd like to invest, you could invest $1,000 in a one-year CD, $1,000 in a two-year CD, and $1,000 in a three-year CD. As each CD reaches maturity, you would have the option of keeping your money in that CD or moving it to some other investment.

If you ladder your CDs, it is important that you keep track of their maturity dates. Banks differ in their policies when it comes to notifying a customer that a CD is about to mature. Typically, a bank will give the owner of a CD only a short period of time to decide whether to roll over the funds from a matured CD; without specific instructions, most banks simply roll the funds over, meaning that the customer's money is reinvested in a new CD with the same term as the mature CD. It's to your advantage, therefore, to work with a bank that gives you plenty of notice that a CD is about to mature so that you have time to decide what to do with the money.

Money Market Account (MMA)

Money market accounts are similar to savings accounts but offer higher interest rates. In general, money market accounts can earn twice the interest that regular savings accounts do. Banks can afford to offer such accounts because they require a higher minimum deposit to open the account. They also require customers to maintain a certain minimum balance. In addition, money market accounts limit the holder to just a few (typically three to six) withdrawals per month. Money market accounts come with check-writing privileges, but the account holder may be limited to as few as three checks per month. Because of these withdrawal limitations, money market accounts are a good place to store funds that you think you'll only need to access occasionally. Because of the combination of higher interest rates and greater liquidity, money market accounts are a good "middle course" between savings accounts and CDs.

Even though money market accounts offer greater liquidity than CDs do, it's important to know that some MMAs are "tiered." With a tiered MMA, the interest rate will vary depending on how much money you keep in the account. In other words, you can take money out of a tiered MMA, but doing so might result in a reduced interest rate. Liquidity, then, may determine what type of account is best for you.

Another consideration is the limitation on the number of checks you can write on a money market account. If you expect to write large numbers of checks, a money market account may not be appropriate. Keep in mind that you can get around check-writing restrictions by using one check to transfer money from your MMA to your regular checking account. Then you're free to write as many smaller checks as you need to.

Money market accounts are offered by banks and by stock brokerage firms. MMAs offered by stock brokerage firms have the advantage of enabling you to invest your funds in stocks, bonds, and other securities. Money market accounts with brokerage firms, though, are not insured by the FDIC. If a brokerage firm gets into financial trouble, its account holders are on their own. On the other hand, money market accounts offered by banks are insured by the FDIC, so account holders face little risk of losing their money. No matter where you have your MMA, it's important to familiarize yourself with any fees the bank or brokerage firm imposes. For example, there may be penalties for exceeding a certain number of transactions in a month; if it happens frequently, your bank may close your account. As with other types of accounts, the lower your balance, the greater the likelihood of getting hit with fees. Some banks will waive fees if you have multiple accounts with them (checking, savings, CD, and so on). If you choose this option, remember that the FDIC will only insure up to $100,000 per depositor, per bank.

WORKSHEETS IN THIS CHAPTER:

· **Record of Savings Worksheet**: Use this worksheet to track the money made and update your balance for your checking, savings, CDs, money market accounts.

Accounts (Checking, Savings, Money Market, etc.)

	Account #1	Account #2	Account #3	Account #4	Account #5
Institution Name					
Contact Name					
Contact Number					
E-mail					
Date Opened					
Account Type					
Account Number					
Amount Invested					
Interest Rate					
Name(s) on Account					

Update 1

Date					
Interest Earned					
Account Balance					

Update 2

Date					
Interest Earned					
Account Balance					

Update 3

Date					
Interest Earned					
Account Balance					

Update 4

Date					
Interest Earned					
Account Balance					

Update 5

Date					
Interest Earned					
Account Balance					

NOTES

INVESTMENTS

Even a casual glance at the business section of a newspaper will show that there are virtually endless ways of investing your money. Many people shy away from investing because they feel intimidated by the array of options available to them. However, such fear is unnecessary. After you've read this chapter, you should have a grasp of the basic concepts of investing.

STOCKS

In the most basic sense, stocks represent partial ownership of a company. Owning part of a company allows you to share in its profits if it makes a profit. Typically, the more profitable a company is, the more a share of its stock is worth.

Stock in most major companies is publicly traded, meaning that anybody who wants to buy shares can do so. Publicly traded stocks are usually bought and sold at a stock exchange, such as the New York Stock Exchange (NYSE). In addition to the NYSE, there are two other major stock exchanges in the U.S.: the American Stock Exchange (AMEX) and the National Association of Securities Dealers (NASDAQ). Stock exchanges serve as a single location at which stocks in thousands of companies are bought and sold by "middlemen" called brokers.

People who own stocks make money off their investment in two ways. One way of making money is if the price of the company's stock rises. In theory, a company's stock price should fluctuate based on how the company is doing financially. As a rule, if a company's products are selling well and it's showing a profit, the price of its stock goes up. Investors may also make money when companies in which they own stock earn a profit. This is because profitable companies typically divide at least part of their earnings among their stockholders, a payment that is known as a dividend.

There are many theories regarding how to make money from stocks. Some experts say that the best way to make money is to buy stock in companies whose business is expected to grow. Stocks of this sort are known as growth stocks. In theory, at least, these stocks will increase in value as the company develops new products or increases sales of existing products. Growth stocks may or may not pay dividends, but in general, those who invest in this kind of stock expect to make money as the price per share of stock increases.

Other experts say that over time, investors are best off if they invest in the stocks of companies that are profitable and are paying regular dividends. Stocks of this type are known as income stocks. As a general rule, income stocks do not fluctuate greatly in price, so investors do not usually expect to make a lot of money selling such stock for a profit.

Most companies issue what is called common stock. Common stock, (also referred to as ordinary shares or common shares) entitles its owner to vote on the company's major business decisions, such as who will sit on the board of directors.

Typically, one vote is allotted per share. In addition, anyone who owns common stock is entitled to attend a stockholders' meeting, which is held once a year. Those who attend that meeting have the right to ask the company's executives how the business is doing. In the event the company goes out of business, those who own common stock receive part of the company's assets—but only after all the company's debts have been paid.

Some companies also issue what is known as preferred stock. This type of stock works differently from common stock, and not every company issues preferred shares. Owners of preferred stock are typically guaranteed a specified dividend, unless the board of directors votes not to pay any dividends at all. Preferred stockholders have no right to vote on a company's decisions. However, if the company goes out of business, preferred shareholders are first in line after creditors to receive a portion of the money that comes from the liquidation of company assets. There are four kinds of preferred stock: cumulative preferred, non-cumulative, participating, and convertible.

Cumulative preferred stock entitles its owner to a cash dividend, or—if the board of directors votes not to pay any dividends—a payment as soon as the company has the cash to do so. Non-cumulative preferred stock is the opposite of cumulative stock, in that the company does not owe the stockholders for the omitted dividends.

The third type of preferred stock is called participating preferred stock. It also pays dividends but with a bonus: should a company have an exceptionally good year, it may pay a special dividend. Holders of participating preferred stock receive this additional payment on top of their guaranteed dividend.

Convertible preferred stock offers an additional option in that at any time, shareholders can convert their preferred shares to a specified number of shares of common stock. Under the right conditions, such as when the price of a company's common stock increases suddenly, converting preferred shares to common shares can be very profitable.

Even though most preferred shares come with a guarantee of a dividend, it's important to remember that investing in stocks is always a gamble. If the price of a stock goes down, you must be prepared to wait for it to recover. Otherwise, you will lose some of what you originally invested. This means that if you anticipate you'll need all the money you're investing, it might be better to put it into a high-yield savings or money market account. At least you will know that the money you started out with is safe.

Because investing in stocks is a gamble, it is particularly important to be cautious if you're considering buying stocks with your retirement funds. Investing in the wrong kinds of stocks can result in significant losses. For example, growth stocks can lose value just as quickly as they gain value. Investors who are in their 20s or 30s can afford to take risks of that sort; but if you are in your 40s or 50s, you should consider buying income stocks or other types of investments altogether.

If you invest in stocks, you'll need to do so through a stockbroker, and that will cost you money. Whenever you buy or sell a stock, your broker will tack on a commission for handling the transaction. You can spend less on commissions by working with a discount broker instead of a full-service broker. If you don't need the research and advice a full-service broker offers, a discount broker might be the best choice.

There is one way to avoid paying a broker's commission altogether, and that is to buy stock in the company where you are employed. Many companies have what are called Employee Stock Ownership Plans (ESOPs). Money is deducted from the employee's paycheck and used to buy stock. Not only do you save money that would otherwise go to a broker but you're assured that your efforts on the job will benefit you because you're now a part-owner of your company.

BONDS

When a large company, city, state, or the federal government wants to borrow money, they may issue bonds. When you buy a bond, you're lending money to whoever issued the bond. The issuer promises to give that money back to you on what is called the maturity date. In the meantime, the borrower promises to pay you interest.

The choices among bonds are almost endless. Bonds vary according to how long they take to mature and when the interest is paid. Of course, bonds differ according to how much interest they pay. For many investors, though, the safety of the bond is what they're most interested in.

Of all the various choices of bonds, the safest are those issued by the federal government. Known simply as government bonds, these securities are backed by the United States Treasury, so investors can be completely confident that the money they're loaning will be repaid. There are many types of government bonds but the ones usually purchased by individual investors are those issued by the United States Treasury Department: Treasury bills (T-bills), Treasury notes (T-notes), Treasury bonds (T-bonds) and U.S. savings bonds. The primary difference between them is how long it takes them to mature. T-bills are the shortest term—they reach maturity within a year. T-notes take the second longest to mature, doing so within one to 10 years. U. S. savings bonds reach maturity after 10 years or more, and T-bonds take 30 years to reach maturity.

Although all four types of government bonds pay interest, the way that interest is paid differs. T-bills are sold at a discount. For example, a T-bill with a face value of $1,000 might be sold to an investor for $950; when the bill matures, the investor gets the entire face value of $1,000. In contrast, T-notes, T-bonds, and U.S. savings bonds are purchased at face value, and interest payments are made in regular intervals along the way.

There is also another type of lesser-known treasury bond: Treasury Inflation-Protected Securities (TIPS). As the name suggests, TIPS protect investors against any rise in the cost of living. As with the other types of government bonds, TIPS pay a fixed interest rate. However, unlike the other bonds, as the cost of living rises, the government adjusts how much principal the investor is owed. The interest payments, since they are based on the principal, go up as well.

TIPS are an extremely safe investment, since you can never lose the money you paid out to begin with. If the cost of living declines, the face value of the bond will decrease, thus decreasing the amount of the interest payments. But at the time of maturity, if the bond's value is lower than the original face value, your original investment will still be returned to you. In other words, you have nothing to lose but some of the interest your investment can earn.

Municipal bonds, which are commonly referred to as "munis," are issued by state and local governments. These bonds pay interest semi-annually. Even though these securities are considered reasonably safe investments, they are not backed by the U.S. government. If the financial managers working for a city or county make poor decisions, the holders of munis may lose their investment. Although it is extremely rare, municipalities have been known to default on their bonds.

Despite this slightly higher level of risk, these securities are quite popular with investors. One feature that makes these securities attractive to investors is that the interest from them is not subject to federal income tax and is often exempt from state and local income taxes as well.

As their name suggests, corporate bonds are issued by companies. These companies use the money they borrow to finance any number of large, expensive projects, such as building a factory. Most of these bonds have terms of a year or longer, and like other bond types, they typically pay interest semi-annually. Unlike state or federal bonds, the interest from corporate bonds is fully taxable on local, state, and federal levels.

Corporate bonds yield high interest rates for two reasons. First, corporate bonds are taxable, so higher interest rates are necessary to offset what investors must pay in taxes. Second, corporate bonds are riskier investments than government or municipal bonds, since there's no government backing for them. If a company goes bankrupt, bondholders are first in line when assets are liquidated, but they rarely see more than a fraction of the bonds' face value.

The highest interest rates are paid on bonds issued by companies whose financial condition is extremely weak. Known popularly as junk bonds, these securities are very risky. Nobody should buy bonds of this sort unless they can afford to lose their entire investment.

Besides the interest they pay, bonds may come with a variety of features meant to make them attractive to investors. For example, some bonds are convertible, meaning that if an investor chooses, the bond can be exchanged for shares of the company's stock. Interest rates on convertible bonds tend to be lower than those on non-convertible bonds, but the potential for making money by converting the bond to stock makes up for that.

Another feature occasionally offered is for a bond to be secured. As the name implies, secured bonds are backed by some sort of collateral. In the event that the company that issued the bond goes bankrupt, money or assets are available to cover the bond's face value. This arrangement ensures that the money invested is returned, making these a popular choice for people who are concerned about the safety of their investment. Most corporate bonds, though, lack this feature.

Although bonds can be a safe and lucrative investment, they become less attractive when interest rates are rising. That's because the bond's owner is locked into whatever interest rate is shown on the face of the bond. There is one kind of bond that addresses this drawback. Known as a "put provision" bond, this type of bond allows the owner to sell it back to the company that issued it before the maturity date and use the money for a different investment.

In general, bonds are most popular in times of low inflation. This is because the interest a particular bond earns usually remains the same, no matter how quickly the cost of living is rising. If you decide to include bonds in your portfolio, you should also include investments that tend to rise in value as the cost of living rises. You might, for example, want to buy some TIPS.

Even though the interest rate on a particular bond is usually fixed, under some circumstances this can work to your advantage. For example, if you buy a bond that pays 6 percent interest, that bond's value increases if interest rates fall. If interest rates drop far enough, buyers might even be willing to purchase the bond from you for more than its face value.

Another variable to consider when investing in bonds is how much you have to pay in commissions. Just as your broker makes a commission from selling stocks, he or she also makes a commission selling certain bonds. Even if a particular corporate bond seems like a safe and lucrative investment, you may find that a government bond with a lower interest rate costs you less to buy. In many cases, the broker's commission on government securities is a modest, flat fee rather than a percentage of the amount you're investing.

INVESTMENTS

MUTUAL FUNDS

Whether you want to invest in stocks, bonds, or some combination of the two, one possible investment is purchasing shares in a mutual fund. A mutual fund is little more than a company formed to allow investors to pool their money. Mutual funds may specialize in stocks, bonds, or other securities; they may also invest in a combination of securities. As the fund's investments increase in value, so does the value of shares in the fund.

One advantage to a mutual fund is that its size reduces the risk of making a bad investment. Because a large number of investors participate in it, the fund can invest in many different stocks, bonds, or other securities at the same time. A professional manager is paid to keep track of how the fund is invested. His or her pay depends on how well the fund's investments do. For this reason, it is in their best interest to make well-researched, educated decisions regarding the fund's investments.

The safety of mutual funds is also helped by close oversight by the federal government. Under the Investment Company Act, which Congress passed in 1940, mutual funds must register with the federal government's Securities and Exchange Commission and report internal operations. The Investment Company Act also requires mutual funds to disclose information regarding how well their investments have done over time, their operating expenses, and their fees. Although there's no protection of the sort that the FDIC provides for bank accounts, not a single mutual fund has ever gone bankrupt since the Investment Company Act was passed.

Most mutual funds allow someone to buy into the fund with an initial investment of as little as $1,000. This feature makes mutual funds an ideal investment for individuals who have not yet built up their savings. Better yet, some mutual funds allow for a "no minimum" investment, as long as the investor agrees to make a regular monthly contribution—which may be as low as $50 to $100. Transaction costs (fees associated with buying and selling securities) are kept to a minimum because securities are bought and sold in very large quantities (sometimes tens of thousands of shares) at a single time.

Not only are mutual funds fairly safe investments they are also fairly liquid. This means that an individual investor can sell his or her shares in a fund, should that need arise.

Mutual funds are either open-ended or closed-ended. Most are open-ended, which means they have an infinite number of shares that can be issued based on demand. An individual investor can buy into the fund by paying at least the minimum amount the fund requires. Open-ended funds also offer investors excellent liquidity, since they can sell their shares back to the company at any time.

Open-ended funds price their shares according to a company's Net Asset Value (NAV). This value is calculated by tallying market value of all the fund's underlying securities, subtracting liabilities, and dividing this by the number of issued shares. As more investors buy into the fund, their money is used to purchase securities. For this reason, adding investors does not cause the value of the fund to decline.

Closed-ended funds operate a little differently. These funds have a finite number of shares, which are bought and sold through brokers. They are traded similarly to shares of stock. Because the shares are finite, their price is determined by supply and demand.

Whether they are closed-ended or open-ended, there is almost no limit to the mutual funds an investor can choose from. An investor can buy into an index fund, bond fund, money market fund, stock fund, hybrid fund, balanced fund, asset allocation fund, or a sector fund. As their names suggest, these funds differ based on what sorts of securities they invest in. Which type of fund is appropriate as an investment depends on the goals of the individual investor.

Index funds tend to be popular among more cautious investors. These funds put their money into securities that are used to calculate one of the popular stock market indexes, such as the S&P 500 Index. Decisions regarding an index fund's investments are usually made using a computer. This means that fees do not have to be paid to portfolio managers or analysts.

Bond funds, as the name implies, invest in bonds. The bonds the funds invest in often have similar dates of maturity, meaning that all of the fund's investments are due to come to term at approximately the same time. Bond funds can be either short-term (maturing within 2 to 3 years), intermediate-term (maturing within 3 to 10 years), or long-term (maturing beyond 10 years). Bond funds provide a stable dividend income while involving a minimal risk.   .

Money market funds are similar to money market savings accounts in that many come with check-writing privileges (although there may be a minimum amount for which the check may be written, typically $250). Money market funds invest in extremely safe things like Treasury bills.

Stock funds (sometimes referred to as equity funds) invest primarily in the stock market. Stock funds fall into either one of two categories, growth funds and value funds. Growth funds tend to invest in companies whose business is increasing rapidly. Much like growth stocks, growth funds primarily invest most of their profits back into the company, meaning that investors do not necessarily receive dividends. Instead, investors make money as the stocks purchased by the fund increase in price. Value funds, on the other hand, focus on the overall soundness of the stocks in which they invest. Value funds typically pay out dividends and offer the potential for long-term, stable growth.

Hybrid funds are made up of several types of securities, typically a mix of stocks and bonds. Hybrid funds may be balanced, meaning that they invest in a fixed combination of bonds as well as common and preferred stock. The stock portion of the fund provides growth, while the bond portion of the fund provides dividend income. Another type of hybrid fund is an asset allocation fund, which varies the mix of bonds and various stocks based on the portfolio manager's expectations of economic trends. Asset allocation funds provide investors with a high level of diversification without having to purchase a number of different funds.

Sector funds are solely invested in a particular economic sector or industry. Sector funds might, for example, specialize in real estate, health care, technology, or any of a number of other industries. Sector funds provide less diversification than any other type of mutual fund, so you risk losing some of your investment if there's a major downturn in the sector such a mutual fund is invested in. On the other hand, if a particular sector of the economy does well, investors in those funds also will also do well.

Sometimes, it's possible to increase your earnings by purchasing a mutual fund that concentrates on investments outside the United States. These types of funds are not hard to spot, as they will usually have words such as international, global, world, or worldwide in their name. Although this type of fund is typically highly diversified in its investments, that doesn't necessarily make it a safe choice. The risks for such funds include currency fluctuations and political instability, factors that can erase the profits from their investments.

No matter what type you decide to invest in, you should consider a mutual fund's previous performance before you select it. Although past performance does not guarantee future performance, it does indicate the overall health of a fund. When researching a fund's performance, it's helpful to look at how the fund performed over the previous 5 to 10 years. *Morningstar Mutual Funds, Value Line Mutual Fund Investment Survey, The Mutual Fund Report*, and *The Mutual Fund Update* are among the sources available to research a fund's history.

In order to make the most out of investing in a mutual fund, it's important to consider whether you're being charged for a commission on your purchase. Some funds, known as load funds, require that a sales commission be paid to the broker who sells you the shares you buy. Commissions can range between 3 and 8.5 percent of the amount invested. Loads can typically be avoided by purchasing a mutual fund directly from the issuing company instead of through a brokerage. Other funds, known as no-load funds, do not pay the broker a commission. By asking ahead of time whether a fund is load or no-load, you can save yourself hundreds or even thousands of dollars.

Whether they are load or no-load, mutual funds often charge their investors other fees. These include expense ratios, which are meant to pay for operating costs and account management. Simply put, fees of this sort cut into an investor's returns. Some mutual funds also charge fees for reinvesting dividends, while others charge a "penalty fee" (also known as a back-end load) if money is withdrawn prior to a certain date. You may not be able to avoid paying such fees, but you can select a fund whose fees are lower than others.

No matter what your financial goals may be, there's a good chance that you can find investments that will help you reach them faster. The key is to research your investments thoroughly and carefully so as to minimize your risk and maximize your gain.

WORKSHEETS IN THIS CHAPTER:

· **Record of Investments Worksheet**: Track the progress and interest accumulated for your stocks, bonds, mutual funds, and more with this worksheet.

RECORD OF INVESTMENTS WORKSHEET

Investments (Mutual Funds, Stocks, etc.)

	Investment #1	Investment #2	Investment #3	Investment #4	Investment #5
Institution Name					
Contact Name					
Contact Number					
E-mail					
Purchase Date					
Account Type					
Account Number					
Amount Invested					
Number of Shares					
Unit Price					
Interest Rate/ Dividend					
Name(s) on Account					

Update 1

Date					
Number of Shares					
Unit Price					
Interest Earned/ Dividends Paid					
Current Yield					

Update 2

Date					
Number of Shares					
Unit Price					
Interest Earned/ Dividends Paid					
Current Yield					

Update 3

Date					
Number of Shares					
Unit Price					
Interest Earned/ Dividends Paid					
Current Yield					

BUYING A HOME

Generations of Americans have grown up believing that they should buy a home just as soon as they have a down payment saved up. But that's not necessarily true. Even if you've got an adequate down payment, there are times when home ownership is not a smart financial move. Experts advise that in general, purchasing a home rather than renting makes sense only if you're planning to own it for at least 4 years. This is because every time you buy or sell property you get hit with expenses like real estate agent's commissions, various fees involving your mortgage, and other miscellaneous charges. Your home is unlikely to gain enough value in less than 4 years to make up for these costs.

The biggest advantage to owning your home can be financial. Yes, you are paying a great deal of interest, but you are also forced to save a certain amount every month. The further along you get in your mortgage, the less you pay in interest and the more you pay off the actual cost of the home, or the principal. Homeownership is one of the best ways to accrue several hundreds of thousands (or even millions) of dollars over a lifetime.

Owning a home has other advantages that are just as important, even if they are not financial. Homeowners feel reassured about their well-being, knowing that they are building a nest egg. They can also decorate and landscape the house any way they want, thereby expressing their identities. Since homeowners are known as responsible, capable members of society, they get an ego boost when discussing their housing situation with others. Individuals derive great pride and satisfaction from owning a home.

Some individuals are convinced they can make such a good return on investments other than real estate that they should rent, rather than buy, a home. They may believe they can save and create more wealth by using their savings and income for other purposes than a mortgage. While it's conceivable that a stock market wiz or business genius can make more money using their cash, most of us cannot claim to be either.

RENTING VERSUS OWNING

Take a look at the following table to get a good idea of where renters come out ahead and where buyers get the sweetest deal. It's a good idea to circle or highlight the advantages most important to you. If you circle more in one column than the other, perhaps that's the best option for you.

FINANCIAL

Benefits of Owning	Benefits of Renting
Part of your monthly mortgage payments go toward building up your equity. You are forced to build up a pool of cash, which you can borrow against in the future.	You don't have to pay for major or minor repairs.
	You don't have to pay property taxes.
You can write off your interest expense on your income taxes. This is the biggest tax write-off available to Americans.	You don't have to pay for costs (thousands of dollars) involved in buying and selling a home.
	Often water, sewer, and other utilities are paid by the landlord, not you.
Your mortgage payment remains steady over the years (if you have a fixed rate and don't refinance and use all of the equity). Rents rise, often yearly.	You don't have to pay most of the insurance costs.
You will have more spending money for your retirement years if your house is paid off.	Since you don't have to put all your cash into a down payment, you have more cash to invest in other areas (such as stocks and bonds) or start your own business.
In the future (15-20 years), your housing expenses will be lower than someone who rents.	
Leverage is used most powerfully in real estate than anywhere else in the investment world. For $20,000, a homeowner can (conceivably and given the right conditions) secure a $400,000 investment. That $400,000 could make a 10% gain in two years or less, netting the investor (borrower) $40,000 on their loan, a 200% return.	

CONVENIENCE

Benefits of Owning	Benefits of Renting
You can do almost whatever you want to your home whenever you want to do it. You don't have to depend on a landlord for maintenance and repairs.	You can move on a whim, with a 30-day notice, provided you don't have a long-term lease. It is fairly easy to find a rental in a short period of time. You can pick up the phone for a repair. With your landlord responsible for maintaining the property, you don't have to worry about lining up repair technicians. There's no worry about falling house values.

INTANGIBLES

Benefits of Owning	Benefits of Renting
Pride in ownership. Status. People who own their own homes are generally viewed as reliable and hard-working. A sense of control over your home decisions. The security that comes from being your own landlord.	Living in close proximity to your neighbors (often sharing common areas such as pools and clubhouses) provides a built-in social network. A feeling of freedom because you aren't tied to one home or place.

TIME SAVINGS

Benefits of Owning	Benefits of Renting
Less time having to move from place to place.	With home repair and renovation, you will spend a fraction of the time researching the home's problem, finding the right repair person, and overseeing the job, compared to a homeowner.

GOOD REASONS TO BUY A HOME

After about 10 years, given a modest inflation rate, the benefits of owning a home start accumulating. At that point, not only are your monthly payments lower than renting but you're building up equity more and more quickly. Your house is your bank. As long as you want to live in it, you can keep depositing money into it.

In case of emergencies, your home can lend you the money in the form of tax-deductible, low-interest second mortgages or home equity lines of credit. That said, most homeowners do their best to keep depositing rather than withdrawing.

THE USE OF LEVERAGE

One of the best reasons to invest in real estate is the leverage that buying a home gives you. Say you invest $25,000 in a down payment on a $500,000 home. You would have a loan of $475,000. In one year, if that $500,000 house increases in value by 10 percent, you would have made a $50,000 profit on your $25,000 investment, or a 200 percent profit. On the other hand, say that you take that $25,000 and put it in the bank earning 5 percent interest. In that same time period (one year), you would have made $1,250. So the real estate investment earned you $48,750 more than if you had left the money in your bank.

Although there are many good reasons for buying a home, there are also bad reasons for doing so. Knowing what those bad reasons are can help you avoid making an expensive mistake.

BAD REASONS TO BUY A HOME

· You're feeling pressure to buy a home. Don't buy when you're not ready financially or emotionally. Make sure you're committed, or you may fall victim to "buyer's remorse."

· Colleagues and peers are buying and you don't want to be left behind. Instead, wait until the market is right and you have the down payment for what you want.

· It's the time of your life when you should have a house. Don't fret. Just because you don't have a house right now doesn't mean you'll never have one.

· Panic. The market is rising and you want to get into something ... anything! Calm your emotions. Markets go up and markets come back down again.

• You think buying will resolve some family issues. Remember, even in the new house the same issues will face you.

Not everyone is ready to buy a home. The following questions will help you decide whether or not you're at a point in your life when purchasing a home makes sense.

• Is the desire to buy a home yours and no one else's?
• Are you willing to keep careful track of mortgage statements, property tax statements, insurance forms, etc.?
• Do you see rent prices in your area rising over the next three years?
• Is your company stable? Is your job secure? If not, will you be able to find another job easily?
• Have you examined your credit and built up a good credit history?
• Do you believe that homeownership is one of the best investments available?
• When you think of repairing sprinklers and patching up wall gouges, do you feel frustrated?
• Do you like going to many stores to find the right drapes, wallpaper, carpets, etc.?
• Do you expect to stay in your area for more than 3 years?
• Do you have several thousand dollars saved up to cover closing costs?
• After paying your current monthly expenses, do you have extra money?

(The costs of owning a home will run a few hundred or even a few thousand dollars more a month than renting.)

If you have answered "no" to any of these questions, consider putting your home-buying plans on the back burner. You can spend some time learning more about real estate, strengthening your credit, and saving money for a down payment. Whatever you do, don't jump into homeownership until you're financially and emotionally ready.

LOOKING FOR A HOME

Once you decide it's time to buy a home, you'll probably want to find yourself a real estate agent. Although it's certainly possible to find and purchase a home on your own, hiring an agent will save you time. Agents have access to a list of most of the homes that are on the market in your area. If you can say clearly what you're looking for in a home, your agent can search that list and find homes that are in your price range and that have the number of rooms and other features you want. When you go looking for an agent, you'll have your choice between using a full-service agent or a discount broker.

Using a full-service agent offers you some distinct advantages. Among other things, a full-service agent will:

- Increase your options. Although you can drive around by yourself, looking at "For Sale" signs and writing down addresses of potential homes, you might miss a side street that has just the right home for you on it.

- Bring you opportunities. Real estate agents often have their ear to the ground and may know about properties even before they officially go on the market. In a hot market, having a real estate agent who's keeping on top of new listings can make the difference between your being the first buyer to make an offer or the third or fourth one to do so.

- Find you the professionals you need to complete your purchase quickly. Usually, your real estate agent can recommend names of mortgage lenders, escrow companies, appraisers, home inspectors, exterminators, and others who are crucial in completing the home-buying process.

- Provide information about the community. Real estate agents can give you information about the local community, telling you about the taxes, schools, hospitals, and local parks.

- Give easy access. It's the agent who will get on the phone and arrange for you to look at a home. You don't have to be the one leaving messages, waiting for a response or calling to follow up.

- Provide experience. Good agents have been through hundreds of homes. They will help you compare the house you are looking at to similar homes.

- Do the dirty work for you. If you don't like confrontation, be sure to hook up with an agent, who will bring your offer to the seller or the seller's agent and negotiate on your behalf.

- Give you more credibility. A seller may take a buyer represented by an agent more seriously. Agents usually pre-qualify buyers and encourage them to get pre-approval from a lender. As a result, sellers know that if a potential buyer is worth the agent's time, he or she is worth the seller's time as well.

- Keep you from missing deadlines. It's the agent's job to keep you apprised of when to sign important documents, when to transfer your funds, when to show up for the home inspection, and when to attend any other important matters.

DISCOUNT REAL ESTATE BROKERS

You can also consider a discount brokerage. Discount brokers have access to the same list of available homes that the full-service agents have; they just aren't going to provide the same level of hand-holding. You may have to drive yourself to the homes you want to look at, and you'll probably have to keep track of the steps in the purchase process yourself. A discount broker, though, will still provide services such as putting you in touch with a mortgage lender. And depending on whether paperwork is handled by escrow companies or lawyers, the broker will link you up with those individuals as well.

COMMON SENSE DEALS

Getting a good deal on a home is much harder than finding a bargain on a new car or pair of jeans. But there are some circumstances where it's possible to hang onto tens of thousands of your hard-earned dollars and still get the home you want. A 6-percent reduction in the asking price of a home is the norm. Under the right circumstances, you might be able to get a significantly greater reduction.

One way of saving money is to look for signs of seller desperation. Real estate agents have a sort of code word for someone who is desperate to sell, which is motivated seller. Sellers get motivated for many reasons. They may be relocating to take a new job and need to buy a home in their new location. They may be in financial difficulty. Or, they simply may be getting tired of seeing a "For Sale" sign in their front yard and want to get the selling process over with. In fact, experts say that if a home has been listed for 60 days or more, you can be certain the seller is getting skittish.

BUY A FIXER-UPPER

Another way of saving money on a home purchase is to buy one that needs some work done on it. During your tour of homes, you will probably come across 1 or 2 that clearly have seen better days. Chipped and scratched paint, stained carpeting, outdated appliances, dull cabinets, and scuffed floors can all be taken care of at a reasonable cost with minimal effort. If you're concerned that you may be buying a home with too many problems, consider hiring an appraiser to give you an idea about the house's value. Usually, an appraisal is done after the sale price has been agreed upon, but you're free to arrange for this sooner. A good appraiser can give you an idea of flaws that might be unknown even to the seller. It's smart to get both the appraisal and the inspection done before you put together your offer. This is not unheard of in the real estate business, and the seller (or at least the seller's agent) will not take offense. You can also bring contractors along and ask for quotes on projected jobs. Use these bids to negotiate a better offer.

LOWBALL YOUR OFFER

If you are not desperate to buy right away, you may consider saving money by making lowball offers. Be ready to lose the home and even risk offending the seller. A lowball offer is generally 20 to 25 percent lower than the asking price or the home's fair market value. If you adopt a lowball strategy, you may make 20 offers on 20 different homes and get just 1 counteroffer and 19 offended sellers. Take heart, you'll probably never see those you've offended again, and the deal you just might get on your home will help you build wealth that much faster.

No matter what strategy you use to save money on a home purchase, keep in mind that home buying is fraught with emotion. If you lose a house, there will be another one that will suit you, perhaps even better. Don't risk making huge purchasing mistakes when you feel rushed or forced to make a quick decision without enough information or time to think.

First and foremost, your concern should be your offering price versus the seller's asking price. After a little negotiating, the two of you will settle on a purchase price. Here are a few things you should know about all 3 figures: the seller's asking price, your initial offering price, and (after a bit of back and forth) the purchase price.

EVALUATING THE ASKING PRICE

Usually, sellers price their homes far higher than fair market value. Often because the agent wants the seller's business, he or she will present a marketing proposal that includes a high price. Owners also tend to view an agent who prices the home high as competent and effective. The perception is that the agent has to be sharp since they recognize the home's great value.

Sometimes the seller won't listen to the agent who is trying to put a fair price on the home. The agent does work for the seller after all, so the agent has to list the home at whatever the seller insists. Overpriced homes may get some showings but few or no offers. Your best bet in such a scenario is to walk away and wait for the price to drop. Eventually, you will find a home you like that is priced more in line with its true value. That's the time to consider making an offer.

THE ART OF MAKING THE OFFER

Agents depend on the prices of homes in the market and those recently sold to come up with a recommendation for an offering price. These comparisons, or "comps," share these characteristics:

- They are on homes located in the same neighborhood.
- They are on homes of the same age, size, and condition.
- The prices are from the past six months.

Keep in mind, though, that the older the comp, the less it reflects fair market value.

In deciding on how much to offer, consider the local economic environment. If a large manufacturer moved out of the area two months ago, the home prices should reflect this current reality. Most likely, "For Sale" signs are cropping up faster than weeds. In a case like this, you can reasonably expect the seller to entertain any serious offer.

DEALING WITH THE COUNTEROFFER

It's fairly common for sellers not to accept the first offer they receive from a buyer. But unless the buyer has made a ridiculously low offer, the seller will probably respond with a counteroffer. It's a good sign when the seller responds with a counteroffer. The seller considered your offer and is willing to work with you. There will probably be a time limit in which you can respond.

If the seller makes a counteroffer, you are free to respond with a counteroffer of your own. You may go back and forth many times before the deal is struck. Try to keep pride out of the negotiations. The seller is not trying to overpower you. Most likely, he or she is just trying to get a fair deal for a beloved home. Giving in on some points will probably end with you getting the home and still feeling like a winner.

Sometimes if the buyer and seller are getting close to agreeing on a price but have stalled, the agent will suggest that you "split the difference." For example, if you're offering $505,000 for a house and the seller states that he will go no lower than $525,000 your agent may advise you to come up $10,000 to $515,000. The seller's agent will similarly advise coming down $10,000. Under such a scenario, both parties have the psychological satisfaction of thinking that they haven't been outmaneuvered by someone more adept. When you split the difference, the final deal feels like a tie.

If you find you're going back and forth to a ludicrous extent, consider pulling out of negotiations. It will give you some time to reassess the house and your decision. It will also give the seller a wake-up call. After you've reassessed the situation and even looked at a few more homes, you are still free to make an offer on the home. By the time you do, the seller may have experienced a long, lonely week without a prospect in sight.

Eventually, if you and the seller will arrive at a mutually agreeable price, you'll sign a sales contract. This document will spell out what you'll pay for the house. It will also spell out just what your money is getting you. If the seller agreed to throw in moveable appliances (such as the washer and dryer), that will be part of the contract. If you agreed that the seller would not have to fix some leaking pipes (a big mistake on your part), that will be noted.

SECURING A LOAN

Now that you've gotten past the negotiations for your house, it's time to find someone who will loan you the money to buy the home you want. Up until the 1970s, almost every homebuyer acquired a 30-year fixed rate loan. More recently, the 30-year home loan has fractured into hundreds of different types of loans, many with strange-sounding names like "piggyback," "hybrid," or "balloon." With so many types of loans available, the lending landscape is like a smorgasbord. You can choose from the buffet of options and find a loan that works for your financial and family situations.

Some homebuyers may need to get in on a reasonable market before prices start going up. Yet their salary is not quite what it will be in 5 years. If you're one of those people, a hybrid loan that has a lower initial fixed rate for the first 5 years and then switches to an adjustable rate after that period could be the best option.

Others who are concerned about the volatility of future rates might want to lock in a reasonable fixed rate at the beginning and coast through the next 30 years, confident that their payment will never change. In a third scenario, the housing market may be so slow that a clever investor cannot resist buying a fixer-upper. If the teaser rate on an adjustable rate mortgage is set at 4.5 percent for 1 year, the investor stands to make good money doing some repairs and renting the home for a year or 2. When the market regains some strength, the investor can consider reselling the home for a tidy profit without having paid too much in interest expenses.

With a little research on your part, you can find the type of loan that most closely meets your needs. Keep in mind, though, that you're going to need to do more than just pay a mortgage each month. A mortgage lender will probably tell you the highest monthly payment that he thinks you are most likely to pay consistently without defaulting. This figure does not take into consideration things like the $200 you want to put into a retirement account each month or the $300 you stash away for your children's college education. Consider your other goals when the lender presents a mortgage figure.

While your agent may recommend a mortgage lender, be cautious. The agent may have fallen into a comfortable relationship with the lender. Remember, even the most knowledgeable real estate agents are not mortgage specialists. They do not have the time to search for the mortgage that's best for you. That job is left up to a mortgage broker.

Before you jump into a loan, take a look at the greater economic forces that drive interest rates. Understand the mortgage terminology your lender or broker sends your way. Ask your lender or broker questions about anything that is unclear. You'll feel more confident and in control when you understand their explanations and are able to use that knowledge in making your loan decision.

As you look over the various loan choices that are available to you, one of your main considerations should be what stage you're at in life. If you go with the law of averages, you will buy your first home at 33, trade up at 44, buy a vacation home at 52, and buy a retirement home at 65. At all of these stages, different financial pressures and rewards exist. Finding the right mortgage for your situation will factor into the balance between your stress and happiness for a long time to come.

CONSIDERATIONS FOR SINGLES

With only one income, it's often hard to come up with a substantial down payment. However, lenders have some flexibility when dealing with home buyers who have limited funds. A few lenders are even willing to consider lending money with very small, or even no, down payment.

If this is your first home, don't forget about Fannie Mae and Freddie Mac programs, which are sponsored by the federal government and offer low down payments and lower interest rate payments to first-time homebuyers. There are certain income ceilings in place to qualify, but if you are beneath them, this is a great way to lock in a low-cost, low-interest loan.

CONSIDERATIONS FOR NEWLYWEDS

Newlyweds are another segment of the population that tends to move quickly, particularly when the children start arriving. Before you buy that first house, have a serious talk with your spouse about what each other's expectations are after the children arrive. Does one of you plan on staying home or working only part-time? When determining how much house you can afford, estimate the income stream at each stage of your lives together, and remember to factor in closing, moving, and other costs.

Keep in mind that even though you're young, you should be building your investments. It's wise, for example, to contribute as much as you can to your retirement plan so that the money can compound over time and build for retirement. That means doing what you can to avoid having to put all your resources into a mortgage payment. Mortgage lenders say that no one ever asks for less than the amount for which they are approved. If you're trying to save for retirement or other goals, be the exception. The maximum mortgage may not be the right one for you. Fannie Mae and Freddie Mac programs might be an option if one of you has never bought a home before.

CONSIDERATIONS FOR FAMILIES

Unlike singles and newlyweds, families tend to stay in a home for a long time. Fixed-rate loans are ideal for this kind of homeowner. With a fixed-rate loan, you'll make the same payment at the beginning of the loan that you'll make at the very end of it. Fixed-rate mortgages almost always have rates that are higher than what an adjustable-rate loan starts at. But if fixed rates are within a percentage point of adjustable rates, the peace of mind involved in a fixed-rate mortgage may be worth the small extra amount of money.

If you have the income to enable you to make the higher payments as an adjustable rate moves up, you might consider going with such a loan. Because rates can adjust down as well as up, in the long run you may end up paying less than if you had chosen a fixed-interest loan.

CONSIDERATIONS FOR RETIREES

It may be appealing to head into retirement debt-free and without a mortgage payment. But think carefully before you pull money out of one of your accounts to pay off the last of your mortgage. If your investments and savings accounts are getting a higher return than the rate you're paying on your mortgage, you're money ahead to keep the mortgage.

Another possibility for some retirees is taking out what is called a reverse mortgage, which is a way for you to gradually take equity out of your home. With a reverse mortgage, the bank gradually pays out money to you. After a fixed period of time, usually 10 to 20 years, the bank has all the equity in your home. Such an arrangement, of course, means that your children or grandchildren will not inherit your home from you.

BEING APPROVED FOR A LOAN

Sometime before you began negotiations for buying your home, you were probably pre-qualified for a loan. This just means that the agent asked you a few questions about your income and assets and then gave you an estimate of how much of a mortgage you could afford. Pre-qualification may give you some idea of which type of loan may work the best for you.

Pre-approval is a more in-depth process than pre-qualification. As part of the pre-approval process, a lender or mortgage broker goes over documents that support what you've stated as your income. These documents may be as simple as the stubs from your most recent paychecks. If you have money in savings and investments, the lender will ask to see statements from the institutions where those accounts are held.

It's important to get pre-approval. In a hot housing market, where there may be two or three people hoping to buy the same house, being pre-approved will assure the seller that the sale will close quickly.

APPRAISALS AND INSPECTIONS

Although lenders may differ in their requirements, it's almost certain that the house you're buying will have to be appraised. All this means is that the lender will hire someone to look at the property and judge whether it's worth at least as much money as you're borrowing. The appraiser will go through the house and verify its size and the type of construction. He or she will then compare the price you're paying against what similar homes in that area sold for. If the appraiser indicates that the home isn't worth the amount of the loan, you may still be approved for the loan if the lender thinks that the property's value is likely to increase. On the other hand, you may have to find a different lender whose lending guidelines are more liberal.

Before the lender issues a mortgage, the property will also need to be inspected for serious flaws. The property inspector will go through the house looking for obvious flaws, such as leaks in the roof, broken or missing smoke detectors, and evidence of termite infestation. Serious problems will need to be fixed before the lender actually issues a mortgage. If a problem is discovered, there's a good chance that you can get the seller to pay for correcting it. At this point, the seller is probably unwilling to see the deal fall apart; he or she is not going to balk at spending even a thousand dollars to have the house fumigated or have the roof repaired.

CLOSING

Once all the paperwork has been completed and any last-minute glitches (yes, there almost certainly will be some!) have been cleared up, the lender will release the money you've borrowed. Depending on the standard procedures in your state, you'll either close escrow or go to an attorney's office to sign all the final documents. At this point, you'll be given the keys to your new home. Now it's time to heave a sigh of relief. You've just made what will probably be your biggest move toward building wealth and assuring your financial future.

NOTES

RETIREMENT PLANNING

Retirement planning is more than dreaming about how you will spend the years after you stop working. Although you will probably be happier in the long run if you have at least a rough idea of what you're going to do with your time, the real purpose of retirement planning is to allow you to have the lifestyle you want without worrying about how you're going to pay your bills. While it is never possible to perfectly plan for the future, you can take important steps to make sure your retirement is comfortable for you and your family.

What you need to remember is that you cannot expect the check you receive from Social Security to cover your needs. In fact, Social Security will only be enough to cover about 30 percent of your living expenses. The rest will have to come from your own savings or from income generated by investments you've made. Even if you're only in your 20s or 30s, now is the time to set up a retirement account and contribute to it regularly.

When it comes to retirement accounts, there are several key numbers to remember.

- 59 – The age at which you may begin drawing from a retirement account without having to pay a tax penalty.

- 10% - The amount of tax penalty you will have to pay the IRS if you withdraw money from a retirement account before you are 59. Certain exemptions do apply, although most people are subject to this rule.

- 70 – With some exceptions, this is the age at which people are required to begin drawing funds from a retirement account. If you do not begin withdrawals by this age, you will be hit with a penalty.

Since the early 1980s, the number of options for retirement accounts has grown dramatically. Today, an enormous array of choices faces anyone who's planning for retirement.

INDIVIDUAL RETIREMENT ACCOUNT (IRA)

An IRA is an account that is opened with a financial institution such as a brokerage firm, bank, credit union, or mutual fund. The federal government encourages people to contribute to IRAs by allowing them to deduct those contributions from their taxable income under certain circumstances. You can make IRA account contributions up to $4,000 per year if you are under the age of 50 and up to $5,000 per year if you are 50 or older.

We know from earlier chapters that stocks, bonds, and mutual funds provide dividend and interest income. Usually, you are required to pay tax on this income. However, earnings on investments that are part of an IRA remain untaxed for as long as they remain in the account. Assuming you've reached age 59, you will only pay tax on the money as you withdraw it.

You have several options available to you in setting up an IRA.

Traditional IRA

Traditional IRAs are geared towards those who believe their taxable income after retirement will be less than or equal to what it is now. If most of your taxable income right now comes from your salary, there's a good chance that once you retire your taxable income will be much lower.

Everyone is eligible to open a traditional IRA and is free to contribute money to that account. If your employer doesn't offer a company-sponsored retirement savings plan (such as a 401k), or if you choose not to participate in such a plan, the money you contribute to your IRA can be deducted from your taxable income. Even if you do participate in a company-sponsored plan, you may be able to deduct at least some of your IRA contribution. Whether or not you are eligible to claim a deduction depends on your income and your marital status. Since the government's rules for who deducts IRA contributions can change from one year to the next, it is important to discuss your particular situation with an accountant or other tax expert.

The money in an IRA is meant to be used for retirement, so it's not a good idea to dip into those funds early. In addition, there are tax consequences if you draw money from your IRA before you are 59. Not only do you have to pay income tax on the money you withdraw but the Internal Revenue Service treats that money as income that you failed to report. You will get slapped with a penalty equal to 10 percent of the amount you withdraw.

Roth IRA

Similar to the traditional IRA, a Roth IRA allows you to contribute certain amounts, depending on your age. Unlike traditional IRAs, however, your contributions to a Roth IRA are not tax-deductible. Instead, once you reach age 59, most if not all of the money you withdraw from the account will not be subject to tax. For this reason, Roth IRAs are well-suited for people who think their income after retirement will be higher than it was before they retired.

As is the case with traditional IRAs, the rules for who can contribute and how much they can contribute are subject to change. It's always a good idea, then, to discuss your particular situation with an accountant. You should also make certain that whoever is working with you to set up a Roth IRA is familiar with details about your income and marital status.

If you have a traditional IRA and you are eligible to open a Roth IRA, it might be to your advantage to convert your account to a Roth IRA. For example, if you've developed substantial sources of income that will continue after you retire, you might want to avoid having to pay tax on your IRA withdrawals. There are systems in place that allow you to convert from a traditional to a Roth IRA. However, this is another area in which you need to meet certain eligibility requirements. Your accountant or tax consultant will be able to tell you if you qualify for a conversion.

There is one last thing to consider prior to making the switch. When you convert your traditional IRA to a Roth IRA, you will have to pay tax on any earnings (gains) and on any original contributions that were deducted from your taxable income. You can use a portion of your IRA to pay this tax, but that money will be treated like an early deduction and you'll be slapped with a 10 percent penalty for using those funds. If you want to know how much money it will cost to convert your traditional IRA to a Roth IRA, conversion tax calculators can be found at websites such as www.smartmoney.com and www.rothira.com.

You can also set up a Roth IRA in addition to your existing traditional IRA. Keep in mind, though, that the IRS does not make any distinctions between IRAs when it comes to limiting contributions to such accounts. Even if you have both a traditional IRA and a Roth, your total contributions will probably not be allowed to exceed the limits for a single IRA. For example, if you are limited to $4,000 in contributions to a single IRA, that will be your limit for total contributions.

Also, remember that you are not allowed to let money sit in a traditional IRA forever. If you do not start drawing from the account after you turn 59, you will eventually be required to take a distribution. In a way, this makes sense: your contributions to a traditional IRA, after all, are only meant to be tax-deferred, not tax-free. Eventually, the government imposes penalties for not making withdrawals. However, Roth IRAs are not subject to required withdrawals. Since you've already been taxed on the contributions to a Roth IRA, you are permitted to leave the money in the account for as long as you choose.

Although IRAs can save you money on your taxes, it's important to consider what sorts of fees you will be charged by whatever financial institution sets up your IRA. Banks, brokerage houses, and similar institutions usually impose at least a modest yearly custodial fee. In addition, if your IRA includes securities such as stocks and bonds, you'll probably be charged commissions on every transaction. As you would with any investment account, you may be able to save money by placing your IRA with an institution that offers discounts on commissions.

SOCIAL SECURITY

Social Security is the federal government's system for helping retirees and those with serious disabilities meet their daily living expenses. In addition to paying benefits to retirees, Social Security pays benefits under a number of other programs. For example, the Supplemental Security Income (SSI) program pays benefits to people who are poor and either retired, blind, or otherwise disabled. Social Security Disability (SSD) benefits are available to people who have some kind of medical condition that will keep them from working for a year or longer. The Social Security program also includes Medicare, which is meant to help retirees and disabled persons pay for their healthcare. Social Security also pays benefits to a spouse (and depending on their age, the children) after the retiree's death. Finally, there are special benefits available to veterans of World War II.

Social Security benefits are primarily monetary and are funded through taxes collected from all American workers and their employers. Specifically, you pay 6.20 percent of your gross earnings in Social Security taxes and 1.45 percent of your gross earnings to fund Medicare.

Retirement Benefits

The largest program within Social Security is the one that pays benefits to people who retire from their full-time jobs. The Social Security Administration says that over 95 percent of American workers are covered by Social Security, which means that when they retire, they will be entitled to at least some benefits. In order to qualify for retirement benefits, you must have worked and paid taxes for at least 10 years.

Your retirement benefit is based on what you earned before you retire, the logic being that the more money you were earning, the more money you and your employer were putting into the system in the form of Social Security taxes. A person may begin receiving at least a partial retirement benefit when they turn 62. That benefit goes up if a worker waits until age 66 (67 for people born in 1960 or later) and goes up even more if someone waits until age 70 to start drawing benefits.

Social Security pays more to people who wait longer to receive benefits. Depending on your income needs and employment situation, you might find it desirable to put off retiring until you reach age 70. Whether you choose to begin receiving retirement benefits at age 62 or at some later age, you should apply for them a few months before you officially retire in order to avoid going without income until they arrive.

Survivor's Benefits

Social Security also pays what are called survivor's benefits. When a person dies, his or her children and spouse are entitled to benefits if:

• The spouse is age 62 or older.

- The spouse is of any age and caring for a child under the age of 16.
- The spouse is of any age and is caring for a child who was disabled before age 22.
- The children are age 18 or younger and not disabled, or over age 18 and were disabled before age 22.
- Children who are age 19 if they are in high school.
- The spouse is divorced but had been married to the deceased for at least 10 years.

Social Security Disability Insurance Program

In addition to providing supplemental income to retirees, Social Security also provides benefits to those with health problems (mental or physical) that prevent them from working. This benefit is extended only to those who meet strict eligibility requirements. People who are unable to work due to drug- or alcohol-related problems, for example, are not eligible to receive benefits.

Whether you can receive benefits depends on your age and how long you've worked. In addition, your disability must be expected to last for at least 12 months, and you must have paid Social Security taxes. The benefits are paid monthly and determined by your average lifetime income. There is a 5-month waiting period from the time a person files a Social Security Disability claim until the time they begin receiving his or her benefit.

A person's family may also receive compensation through Social Security. Qualifying family members include children (biological, from adoption or remarriage, and sometimes grandchildren) who are age 18 or over and were disabled prior to age 22; and, a spouse who is over age 62 or is taking care of your child who is disabled or under age 16.

Unlike retirement benefits, Social Security Disability benefits are not paid to the former spouse of a disabled person, regardless of how long they were married.

Medicare

Most Americans over age 65 are covered by Medicare. At the most basic level, this program is health insurance for retirees and people with disabilities. Those covered by Medicare get help paying for visits to their doctor, hospital stays, and other medical services.

Medicare also provides insurance to cover purchases of prescription medicines. The law that established this drug insurance is extremely complex and provides for a wide array of plans. Your financial situation determines how much any one plan's coverage costs. One thing to remember, though, is that the government requires people to join some kind of prescription insurance plan when they qualify for other Medicare coverage. There are penalties for waiting too long to sign up for prescription drug coverage.

Not everyone qualifies for Social Security benefits. For example, those who continue to work and earn more than amounts set by the Social Security Administration are not entitled to benefits. If someone chooses to work part-time, the government uses a sliding scale to determine how much money they receive from Social Security.

Family members and survivors are also subject to limitations on income in order to receive benefits. These limits are revised periodically, so it's always a good idea to check with the Social Security Administration to see how much you can earn before benefits are reduced or eliminated altogether.

The Social Security Administration has strict formulas for calculating how much it pays in benefits. However, you can take steps to make sure you make the most of what Social Security has to offer. This is especially true when it comes to Medicare. For example, Medicare covers most retirees for hospitalization, but visits to your doctor are not covered unless you buy extra insurance—what's known as Medicare Part B. This extra insurance is a good value, since it costs just a fraction of what comparable health insurance costs people who are not old enough to qualify for Medicare.

KEOGH PLANS

A Keogh plan is for the small, self-employed business owner and his or her employees. Like an IRA, it is a tax-deferred retirement savings program. However, Keogh plans offer substantial tax benefits far beyond what an IRA provides.

Keogh accounts come in two types. One is known as defined benefit (also called a money purchase plan). This type of Keogh allows you to choose a specific amount you want to receive in benefits when you retire. How much you pay in is based on a mathematical formula that takes into consideration a participant's age when the plan is set up, his or her life expectancy, retirement benefit amount, and the number of years until retirement. An annual contribution is mandatory and the same percentage of your income must be contributed each year.

The other type of Keogh plan is called a profit sharing plan, because it takes into account the profits a business earns. This type of plan can be helpful if your business's income fluctuates from one year to the next. If your business has an unprofitable year, you do not have to make payments into the plan at all.

The advantage of Keogh plans is that they have high maximum contributions, meaning you can build up a large balance in your account as your business thrives. Money purchase plans allow for tax-deductible contributions of 25 percent of your annual income, or $40,000, whichever is less. Keogh contributions and their gains are exempt from taxation as long as they remain within the account. Much like other types of retirement accounts, funds deposited into a Keogh can be invested in various ways, including stocks, bonds, and mutual funds.

Not only do Keogh plans allow you to set aside more money than any other type of retirement plan but participation in a Keogh plan has no effect on your ability to participate in an IRA. If you are self employed and have the means to open some kind of IRA in addition to your Keogh plan, you are free to do so.

Participants in Keogh plans are required to start withdrawing money from the account within one year of retirement or when they reach the age of 70, whichever comes first. As is true of a traditional IRA, if you choose to withdraw money from the account prior to 59, you will be hit with a penalty.

Keep in mind that because you deferred paying taxes on your Keogh contributions, you will be taxed on what you withdraw. This means that if you unexpectedly find yourself with other taxable income, you may owe the IRS more money than you planned on.

401(K) PLANS

As the twentieth century drew to a close, fewer and fewer employers were offering their workers traditional pension plans. Instead, with the blessings of the federal government, employers increasingly offered 401(k) plans. Under these plans, employees agree to have a portion of their earnings deposited in a tax-deferred account. Money in the account is then invested so that the balance will grow. Like other investment accounts, money in a 401(k) can be used to purchase stocks, bonds, or other securities.

401(k) contributions are usually not defined as specific dollar amounts. Instead, employees specify a percentage of their earnings to be set aside in the 401(k). The government's rules regarding how much of your income can be set aside in a 401(k) plan are subject to change, but the limits are considerably higher than those placed on IRAs. There's a good chance that your employer's payroll department can advise you on how much you can contribute.

One feature that distinguishes 401(k) plans from traditional IRAs and makes them popular is that many companies match their employees' contributions. This means that as you contribute to your retirement plan, so does your employer. The amount that an employer contributes to an employee's 401(k) varies from company to company. One common formula, though, is a 50 percent match, meaning that for every dollar the employee contributes, the employer contributes 50 cents. Usually, employers cap the amount they will match at around 6 percent of your annual salary.

Depending on your employer's policies, you may have some choice in how much control you have over how your 401(k) funds are invested. You get the most control with what are known as participant-directed plans. Under this type of 401(k) plan, the individual employee has some control over how funds in the account are invested. People who are confident of their knowledge of investments like these plans because they get to personally decide how to make their retirement fund grow.

If you want to control the investments in your 401(k), it's important to remember that transactions can cost you money in the form of fees and commissions. At the very least, it makes sense to ask in advance how much a particular transaction is going to cost. For example, buying U.S. Treasury securities is usually cheaper than buying stocks.

Some companies offer their employees what is called a trustee-directed plan. With this type of plan, a board of trustees decides where the individual participant's assets are invested. If you are uncomfortable dealing with investments and your employer offers a trustee-directed plan, you will likely want to consider this as an option.

Some people worry that even if they have maximum control over their 401(k), they could lose all their money if their employer goes bankrupt. But such an event is unlikely. A federal law called The Employment Retirement Income Security Act (ERISA) protects accounts by requiring that all 401(k) funds be held in custodial accounts that the company cannot access. Although a company can go bankrupt, its employees' money is safe.

Although federal law protects 401(k) accounts in the event of a bankruptcy, it does not protect you from making poor investment choices. Therefore, if you choose a participant-directed 401(k), it is important to avoid putting all of your funds into one type of security. That even applies to investments in your own employer's stock. For example, when companies such as Adelphia and Enron went bankrupt, stock prices fell from $90 per share to less than $.30 per share nearly overnight. Employees who had the bulk of their 401(k) investments tied up in company stock lost hundreds of thousands of dollars and have little hope of recovering that money. In fact, investment experts recommend putting no more than 10 percent of your funds into your own employer's stock.

Although 401(k) accounts are designed to be a secure way of saving for retirement, some companies allow their employees to borrow against their 401(k) accounts. Federal regulations permit this kind of borrowing and allow up to 50 percent of the balance in an employee's account 401(k) or $50,000, whichever is less. But this loan comes with strings attached – the amount borrowed will have to be repaid with interest. If you don't repay the loan within the time specified by the IRS (usually 5 years), the money you borrowed is treated like an early withdrawal. You will have to pay tax on what you've borrowed and also pay a 10 percent penalty. The IRS is a bit more lenient if the money borrowed from the 401(k) is used as a down payment on a home. Typically, people are given 15 to 20 years to pay back the loan in this situation.

Whatever your purpose in borrowing from your 401(k), there's a catch: in the event you are fired or laid off, that loan must be repaid within 60 days. If you are unable to pay within that time frame, the IRS will tax the outstanding balance and you'll be forced to pay an additional 10 percent penalty.

If you do leave your job, it's important that you leave your money in some kind of retirement account. If you spend the money or put it into a regular investment or bank account, you'll have to pay taxes and hefty penalties. Fortunately, you have a couple of options for what to do with your 401(k):

· Have your former employer transfer your 401(k) to your new employer's retirement plan.
· Have the balance transferred into an IRA.
· If the current value of your investment is over $5,000, you have the option of leaving the money where it is. Although you will not be able to make further contributions and your former employer will no longer be contributing money to the account, it will still be able to grow through whatever investment options you have chosen.

Some employers offer a different option: a Roth 401(k). As the name implies, this is a hybrid of the Roth IRA and traditional 401(k) plans. Roth 401(k) accounts let you take money from earnings that have already been taxed and set it aside, just as you do with a traditional 401(k). But once you retire the money that comes out of the account will be exempt from taxation because taxes were paid before the money went into the account.

A Roth 401(k) sounds like a winning combination, and for many people it is. Employees who are just joining the workforce can almost always benefit from opening a Roth 401(k). That's because someone who's just entering the workforce is almost certainly in a lower tax bracket than someone who's been working for 10 or 15 years.

Although investing in Roth 401(k)s often makes sense, you must think carefully about what your future earnings are likely to be. If you expect to have substantial income that will continue even after you retire, the Roth option makes sense, since withdrawals from that account won't be taxed. On the other hand, if you anticipate having relatively little taxable income after you retire, contributing to a traditional 401(k) and paying taxes when you withdraw the money could be the better choice. As you consider the pros and cons of a traditional versus a Roth 401(k), keep in mind that the IRS requires holders of either type of 401(k) to begin withdrawing money at age 70.

No matter what type of account you end up choosing as you plan for retirement, remember that the key to assuring a secure, comfortable retirement requires discipline. That means committing yourself to making regular contributions to your retirement account, even if that means reining in day-to-day spending.

NOTES

PERSONAL CREDIT

Simply stated, credit is a measure of a person's financial trustworthiness. Our credit reflects how we have handled payments on credit cards and loans for cars, homes, and other items. People who have made their payments in a timely fashion have good credit. As a result, banks and other lenders are more likely to make other loans to them. Having good credit can even make a difference when someone is deciding whether to rent an apartment to you or offer you a job. And when a bank is deciding what kind of interest rate to charge you on a mortgage, having good credit is likely to get you the lowest possible rate. In this and other ways, your personal credit impacts your ability to save money and build wealth.

Your personal credit record reflects more than how you have handled your credit cards. It contains information about your checking and savings accounts, any car or mortgage loans in your name, even whether you have ever taken out loans to pay for school. Your credit score, then, is like a snapshot that someone who has never met you will use to get a sense of who you are.

HOW YOUR CREDIT SCORE IS DETERMINED

Everyone who has ever bought anything with something other than cash has a credit history on file somewhere. There are three companies that make a business of keeping track of personal credit: Equifax, Experian, and Trans Union. Their job is to use a person's personal financial history to calculate the likelihood that this individual will make good on his or her loans. To do this, they use a mathematical model developed by the Fair Isaac Company (often referred to as FICO). This model determines a person's credit worthiness using a point system. The sum of these points is known as your credit score. The scores vary widely, from 300 to 850, with the national average score being 678.

The first thing the FICO model looks at is your payment history. This makes up 35 percent of your credit score. If you have paid your bills on time, that helps raise your FICO score. On the other hand, if you have a history of being delinquent with your payments, you will receive a low score. If your accounts have been turned over to collection agencies, your score will be even lower. If you've ever declared bankruptcy, you will be assigned the lowest FICO score for payment history.

The FICO model also looks at the way you've used the credit you already have available. Specifically, FICO considers how much money you owe to creditors in relation to how much you could potentially borrow. This number accounts for 30 percent of your FICO score. Consumers who have a substantial amount of credit available—for example, those who have lots of different credit cards—get a relatively low score, even if they owe nothing on those cards. The logic FICO uses is that people with a lot of credit available are likely to use it, and therefore may let their spending get out of control.

FICO looks at more than how large your line of credit is, however. More important than how much credit you have is how much debt you have in relation to that credit. For example, consider two consumers, Jill and John. Jill owes $1,000 on a credit card that has a $10,000 limit. Because she owes little in relation to how much is available to her, she will likely receive a high score. But John owes $4,000 on a credit card with a $4,500 limit. Even though John's credit line is less than Jill's, he will receive a lower score because his ratio of debt to available credit is higher. Experts say that to receive a good credit score, it's important for your debt not to exceed 25 percent of your available credit.

Your payment history and available credit together accounts for 65 percent of your FICO score. An additional 15 percent of your score comes from how long you've had credit. People who have just recently gotten credit are considered a higher risk than people who have had it for a long time. What matters to FICO, then, is not just how reliably you've paid your bills, but how long you've shown yourself to be reliable.

In addition, 10 percent of your score is related to how many times you've asked for credit. If you have made multiple applications for credit in a short period of time, you will be considered a higher risk than a person who applies for credit infrequently. Finally, your credit mix accounts for another 10 percent of your score. People who have had several types of lines of credit—such as car loans, credit cards, and a mortgage—tend to receive higher FICO scores than those who have only one kind of credit available.

THE CONSEQUENCES OF BAD CREDIT

Your credit score not only affects whether or not you'll get a loan but also affects the interest rate you'll be offered. If your credit score is low, you will be considered "high risk" and will therefore be charged a premium interest rate. In other words, someone may only be willing to loan you money if the incentive for taking that risk is great enough.

Potential lenders, landlords, and employers are not the only ones who take a peek at your credit report. You should be aware that insurance companies are also among those who consider your credit rating. This is because someone who has proven responsible about their use of credit is likely to be responsible in other ways. Companies that sell auto, homeowners, and health insurance may base the premiums they charge (at least partially) on your credit rating. Some companies will deny an insurance application based on your credit history alone.

FIXING YOUR CREDIT

If you suspect your credit score is shaky, you should first obtain a copy of your credit report so you know exactly which areas to tackle. The addresses, phone numbers, and web addresses for the three credit agencies are listed below.

Equifax
PO Box 740241
Atlanta, GA 30374
(800) 685-1111
www.equifax.com

Experian
PO Box 2104
Allen, TX 75013
(800)-682-7654
www.experian.com

Trans Union
760 W. Sproul Road
Springfield, PA 19064
(800) 888-4213
www.TUC.com

Each company allows you to purchase their credit report along with your FICO score. The charge for individual reports is usually between $12 and $15. Everyone, though, is legally entitled to a free copy of their credit report from each agency once every 12 months. Equifax, Experian, and Trans Union have created a centralized service (called AnnualCreditReport.com) that allows consumers to view and print their credit reports online. It is also possible to request copies via telephone or mail:

Annual Credit Report Request Service
PO Box 105281
Atlanta, GA 30348
(877) 322-8228
www.annualcreditreport.com

This service does not provide consumers with a free copy of their FICO score, though. To get the free report, you need to contact the individual credit-reporting companies.

Experts say that it's important for individuals to check the accuracy of the information on their credit report. The credit-reporting companies and the creditors themselves frequently make errors. Even the most basic information may be incorrect. There may be one or more misspellings of your name, an incorrect Social Security number, or an incorrect driver's license number listed. Someone else's information may even wind up on your report.

Your credit report will contain specific information on how to go about disputing and correcting errors. If you do find that someone has made an error, you will need to contact the reporting company. This should be done in writing and, if possible, by certified mail, so you will have proof that the letter was received. You should include an explanation for why you are disputing the information and request that it be either corrected or removed altogether. Be sure to keep copies of correspondence in the event you need it in the future.

Credit-reporting companies will take requests for correction over the phone, but if you decide to take that step, be sure to take notes on the conversation. Write down the date and time of the call; make a note of the name of the person with whom you spoke so that you can make sure the problem has been remedied. By law, credit-reporting companies are required to respond to a request to correct errors within 30 days. However, it may take between three and six months to actually have mistakes corrected.

Even if you find that your credit report accurately contains some negative information, take heart – bad marks on your credit report will not stay there forever. The Fair Credit and Reporting Act of 1971 requires that negative information on your credit report be removed after a specified period of time. For example, a bankruptcy must be wiped off your report 10 years after it was entered. Records of lawsuits, tax liens, and judgments are supposed to be removed after 7 years. But sometimes that doesn't happen. If you see something on your credit report that should have been removed, you will need to contact the credit-reporting companies to request the removal.

Even if you have some fairly recent blemishes on your credit report, you may be able to improve your overall credit score. For example, because your payment history makes up 35 percent of your total credit score, you can greatly improve your credit score by bringing all your accounts up to date. If you are able to pay off your balances entirely, that's even better. Last, if you are in the process of trying to improve your credit rating, you should refrain from making any additional applications for credit. Since 10 percent of your FICO score relates to how many times you have applied for credit, continuing to do so will only further reduce your overall score.

BUILDING CREDIT

Because your credit score depends to a large extent on how you've used available credit, it's important to establish credit in the first place. Since one of the things you will be judged on is how long you have had relationships with lenders, the sooner you establish such relationships, the better.

Your bank or credit union is a good place to start. Oftentimes, they offer customers what's known as a secured credit card. Secured credit cards look just like any other credit card, but they're tied to a bank account with money in it. Your credit limit will be equal to the balance in the account. As long as you pay off the charges you've made on the card each month, that deposit won't be touched. Using a secured card will allow you to establish a payment history.

Another good way to establish credit is to apply for a credit card issued by one of the major oil companies and use it to purchase fuel for your car. Oil companies are usually willing to issue such cards because the available line of credit may be as little as $500, and the items that can be charged are generally not expensive. Similarly, large department stores sometimes issue their own credit cards. Because these cards have small credit limits and are only good in certain stores, they tend to be relatively easy to obtain.

When you open a credit account, charge small amounts on each card and try to pay off the balance every month. If you are unable to pay the whole balance, be sure to send at least the minimum payment. You must also be sure to pay other bills on time. Late payments on household utilities, phone bills, or car insurance can wind up on your credit report. Remember, your payment history makes up 35 percent of your credit score.

Remember that being cautious with your spending will help you boost your credit score. If you develop a habit of running up large balances, creditors may become worried that you'll soon start having difficulty paying your bills. On the other hand, if you are mindful of your spending, diligent with your payments, and minimize the amount of money you owe, it will be easy to achieve and maintain a high credit score. The result will be easier access to the lowest available interest rates when you most need them.

NOTES

DEBT

By the time people reach their early 20s, it is likely they are familiar with the concept of debt. Simply put, debt consists of what you owe other people or institutions. Debt comes in all shapes and sizes, ranging from the $10 you borrow from a friend at lunch to the mortgage you take out to purchase a home.

GOOD DEBT, BAD DEBT

Financial experts classify debt in two categories: good debt and bad debt. Good debt is defined as debt that will improve your overall quality of life. Education loans are a prime example of good debt. Although attending college can be expensive and result in a substantial level of debt, over time the earnings of someone with a college degree will be far greater than the cost of getting that degree. It's worth noting that the time it takes for a college degree to pay for itself is relatively short. On average, college graduates earn $20,000 per year more than those who only have a high school diploma.

Real estate loans are also considered to be good debt. Historically, real estate has proven to be a sound investment because the property increases in value over time. For example, the home you purchase for $200,000 today may be worth $250,000 in several years. Loans on real estate that is purchased and then rented to someone else can be an even better form of debt. If the rent someone charges on a property is higher than the monthly mortgage payment, the tenant is essentially helping pay the mortgage even as the value of the property increases. These are just a few of the reasons why real estate loans are considered to be good debt.

On the other hand, bad debt consists of loans taken out for items that are consumable or that decrease in value over time. Credit-card debt is a prime example. People often use credit cards to purchase vacations, meals, and other consumable items. It is particularly unproductive to go into debt for items that are quickly consumed. Such purchases soon lose their value, and if you don't pay off the credit card every month, the interest on the unpaid balance makes purchases even more expensive.

Experts don't say that "bad" debt needs to be avoided altogether. What most financial advisors say is that a person's bad debt should be less than 20 percent of their annual take home pay. For example, if you make $50,000 a year after taxes, it would be wise to keep the total of your bad debt below $12,000. By keeping your bad debt to a minimum, you can enjoy financial peace of mind when it comes time to pay your bills every month.

ELIMINATING DEBT

Unless you win the lottery, it will be difficult for you to get out of debt overnight. You will need to make regular payments to your creditors; at the same time, you'll need to meet your daily living expenses. Getting out of debt requires time, patience, and commitment.

The first step to tackling your debt is making a commitment to reduce unnecessary expenses. That will leave more of your disposable income to go toward repaying your creditors. (See Chapter 3 for more on how to reduce your spending.) Once you eliminate unnecessary spending, you must also commit yourself to putting this extra money toward paying off your debts.

To get out of debt, you will need to make more than the minimum payment shown on your billing statements. The minimum payment on most credit cards, for example, is usually a very small portion of the total balance (usually just 2.5 percent). Most of your payment, in fact, goes toward paying interest on the balance. Paying more than the minimum allows you to start attacking the principal of your balance, and along the way this saves you hundreds, even thousands, of dollars in finance charges. For example, let's say that you purchase a new washer and dryer for $1,500, using your credit card. If you make a minimum monthly payment, it can take you more than 16 years to pay off the original balance. In addition, you will have paid more than $1,800 in interest, more than the cost of the appliances themselves!

Once you have created room in your budget to make larger payments to your creditors, start by paying off your highest interest loans first. In other words, a credit-card balance with a 20 percent APR should be paid off before one that has an 11 percent APR. And a card with an 11 percent APR should be paid off before your 7 percent APR car loan. Thinking through your payment priorities will not only help reduce your debt but also save you from paying unnecessary interest.

A second option is to call your creditors to negotiate a lower interest rate. A lot of people are unaware that customer service representatives for credit-card issuers are authorized to do this. Since it's usually possible to move balances from one card to another, you might well be able to convince a credit card company to accommodate you with a lower rate rather than lose you to a competitor.

If you are unable to negotiate a better rate, you can consider going ahead and transferring the balance to a new card that carries a lower rate. Taking advantage of balance transfer offers can save you from paying exorbitant interest charges and also help you pay off your balance more quickly. Keep in mind, though, that such a tactic should be considered a last resort. Having too many credit cards, after all, will cause your credit score to drop.

If you do choose to open a new credit-card account, be sure to read the fine print and familiarize yourself with its terms and conditions first. Quite a few credit-card issuers offer low introductory APRs but raise them significantly after six months. For example, your new card with the 1.9 percent APR might soon charge you a 23 percent APR. Also, it is especially important to make on-time payments with these cards. If you are late or miss a payment, you may forfeit the introductory rate even sooner. In any case, transferring your credit-card balance to a new card only makes sense if you expect to pay off the balance before the introductory period expires.

Another way to get control of your debt is to close accounts you rarely use. Although holding several types of accounts can boost your credit score, you don't need 5 gas cards, 3 department store cards, and 6 credit cards to accomplish that. After you have paid down your account balances, close the ones you don't need. Be certain to ask the company's customer service representative to mark the account as having been "closed at the customer's request" so as to keep your credit report accurate.

Another way to pay down debt is to use the assets you already have. If you own a home, for example, taking out a home-equity loan can be one way to get the cash to pay off a high-interest credit card balance. Home-equity loans typically have lower interest rates (usually under 10 percent) than credit cards have. In addition, the interest you pay on a home-equity loan is tax deductible. However, if you take out a home-equity loan to pay down credit-card debt, resolve to make changes in your spending habits. Taking out one loan to pay another will solve very little if you run up your credit-card balances again.

Finally, look into whether you have enough in your savings that could help eliminate or reduce your debt. Whatever APY your savings accounts, money market accounts, CDs, and mutual fund accounts may be offering you, the income you receive from these accounts is probably less than what you're paying in credit-card interest. You should never completely wipe out your savings for such a purpose. It is always a good idea to have money set aside for emergencies. However, if you have additional funds, it makes sense to use them to pay down whatever debts carry the highest interest rates.

MANAGING YOUR DEBT

Of course, with proper management, your debt should not build up to the point where you need to draw on your hard-earned assets to pay it off. The best way to manage your debt is to pay your bills on time. Some creditors allow you to set up a system to automatically deduct payments from your checking account each month. This option will ensure that you are never late for or miss a payment.

If you want to continue to mail your payments, keep in mind that you need to mail them early enough to ensure that they will arrive by the due date. There are tools available to help you do this; many credit card issuers, for example, will send you an email reminder that your bill is due within the week. Visit the websites of your creditors to sign up for bill-pay reminders and other features that help make paying your bills fast and easy.

If you find you are going to be late with a payment, call your creditor as soon as possible and explain the situation. Oftentimes you will be able to make the payment over the phone. Although you will likely be charged anywhere from $10 to $20 for this service, the phone payment charge is likely to be less than the penalty assessed for late payment (which can run anywhere from $25 to $40). You can also call your creditors to let them know that a payment is in the mail. Sometimes, they will make a note on your account that the payment is forthcoming and hold off on assessing a penalty.

Being indebted is certainly a heavy burden and one that many Americans share. But by routinely assessing your finances, budgeting carefully, and staying on top of your credit-card balances, you can get control of your debt before it gets control of you.

WORKSHEETS IN THIS CHAPTER:

- **Credit Card Information Worksheet:** Use this handy worksheet to keep record of your credit cards, their expiration dates, your charge limits, and useful contact information in the event that a card is lost, stolen, or must be replaced. Staying organized is an important step to becoming financially stable.

- **Debt Elimination Worksheet:** This worksheet will help those in debt get a better idea of what they owe on their credit cards, loans, medical bills, legal bills, and other areas of expense. By recording your monthly balances and amounts paid, you can determine your constant progress toward paying down your debts.

- **Determining Debt Payments Worksheet:** This chart allows you to keep track of your creditors and your monthly payments toward these debts. Use the **Monthly Budget Worksheet** in Chapter 2 to determine your Ready Income, or the income you have available to pay down your debts.

Company Name	Card Number	Expiration Date	Charge Limit	If Lost or Stolen... (phone number & address on back of card)
		/	$	
		/	$	
		/	$	
		/	$	
		/	$	
		/	$	
		/	$	
		/	$	
		/	$	
		/	$	
		/	$	
		/	$	
		/	$	
		/	$	
		/	$	

DEBT ELIMINATION WORKSHEET

		Loans			Credit Cards		
	Creditor Name						
	Account Number						
	Balance Due						
	Interest Rate						
	Contact Info.						
JAN.	Interest/Fees						
	Amount Paid						
	Balance Due						
FEB.	Interest/Fees						
	Amount Paid						
	Balance Due						
MARCH	Interest/Fees						
	Amount Paid						
	Balance Due						
APRIL	Interest/Fees						
	Amount Paid						
	Balance Due						
MAY	Interest/Fees						
	Amount Paid						
	Balance Due						
JUNE	Interest/Fees						
	Amount Paid						
	Balance Due						
JULY	Interest/Fees						
	Amount Paid						
	Balance Due						
AUG.	Interest/Fees						
	Amount Paid						
	Balance Due						
SEPT.	Interest/Fees						
	Amount Paid						
	Balance Due						
OCT.	Interest/Fees						
	Amount Paid						
	Balance Due						
NOV.	Interest/Fees						
	Amount Paid						
	Balance Due						
DEC.	Interest/Fees						
	Amount Paid						
	Balance Due						

Personal			Other			Total

DETERMINING DEBT PAYMENTS WORKSHEET

Creditor	Balance Due	÷	Total Debt*	=	% of Total Debt	×	Ready Income**	=	New Payment
(Example) Visa	$425	÷	$4,650	=	9.14%	×	$925	=	$84.54
(Example) Student Loan	$250	÷	$4,650	=	5.38%	×	$925	=	$49.73

* Total Debt: Use the *Debt Elimination Worksheet* to find the cumulative amount of debt you owe to all creditors.
** Ready Income: Is the amount of money you have ready to pay off debt. Determine your budget on the *Monthly Budget Worksheet* then calculate your remaining Ready Income.

TAXES

For generations, people have accepted the wisdom of Benjamin Franklin when he said, "Nothing is certain but death and taxes." And while we still must accept the inevitability of death, it is almost certainly possible to reduce the amount of money you pay in taxes. That's especially true when it comes to income taxes.

There's a good chance that you start paying income taxes your first day on the job. In fact, one of the first forms you fill out when you report to a new job is what's known as a W-4. The information you provide on this form is used by your employer to figure out how much to deduct from your paycheck for federal, state, and local income tax.

You employer keeps careful track of how much money has been withheld from your check for taxes, and shortly after the end of the year, you'll receive another form called a W-2, which shows how much pay you received and how much was withheld for taxes. It's then your responsibility to file your tax return with the Internal Revenue Service (IRS). On that return you'll report all your income. You'll also have to calculate the tax on that income. If your employer has withheld more tax than you actually owe, you'll get a refund; if too little tax was withheld, you'll have to make up the difference.

All this sounds easy and straightforward, but except for a lucky few, it's not. The tax laws are extremely complex, so much so that Americans pay many millions of dollars to experts who understand the ins and outs of the tax code. Much of what we pay these experts to do involves filling out our tax forms and keeping what we pay in taxes to a minimum.

If you are young and your only income is from your salary, there's a good chance that you can file your own taxes. The return you fill out will probably only amount to a page or two. The IRS provides a fairly simple table that you can use to figure out what your tax obligation is.

When it comes to filing income taxes, though, such simplicity quickly vanishes as soon as you try to reduce your tax obligations. You'll need to have all the proper forms at hand; you'll need to have all the receipts and documents that show deductible expenses close at hand; and (perhaps most crucial) you'll need blocks of time in which you're left undisturbed while you add up everything and fill out the forms.

If you're like most of us, you'll begin the process of calculating your taxes by determining your gross income. Your gross income consists of your salary plus any additional sources of income, such as a side business or interest and dividends from investment accounts. Once you determine your gross income, you subtract any and all adjustments. Examples of adjustments include moving expenses, student loan interest, and contributions to traditional IRAs. After subtracting these amounts from your gross income, you will arrive at your Adjusted Gross Income (AGI).

After your AGI is determined, you will be able to subtract either a standard deduction or itemized deductions. If you itemize—that is, add up the various categories of deductible expenses—you'll also have to fill out Schedule A, on which you detail what your expenses were. Once that is done, you will subtract personal exemptions. The final number will equal your taxable income.

The amount of the standard deduction depends on a number of factors, including whether you're single, are the head of a household, or married. You'll also be able to take additional deductions for having dependents, being blind, or for being over age 65. Some of these deductions can be substantial—in excess of $10,000. It will be up to you, though, to figure out what deductions you qualify for. If you miss a deduction and discover it later, you'll have to file additional paperwork in order to reduce your taxable income.

If you decide to itemize your deductions, you'll need to go through the various receipts and reports that you should have been filing away over the previous year.

Examples of itemized deductions include:

- Medical and dental expenses
- Home mortgage interest deductions
- Charitable contributions
- Losses due to casualty, disaster, and theft
- Education expenses
- Business entertainment expenses
- Business travel expenses
- Business use of your home
- Business use of your car

Individuals vary when it comes to deciding how aggressive to be in claiming itemized deductions. Since it can be very difficult to place a value on things like clothing donated to a homeless shelter, for example, individual taxpayers may be tempted to inflate the value of such contributions. Some taxpayers also are generous with themselves in calculating what sorts of expenditures really were business-related. Being aggressive in taking such deductions has its risks, of course. If the IRS denies a deduction, the taxpayer gets hit with back taxes and penalties.

When and if you itemize deductions, it is important to remember that if the IRS questions any deduction, you will need to show proof of that expense. Some tax experts say that unless you have a receipt to back up any deduction, it is unwise to take it. The IRS can revisit your returns for up to three years after you file them, so you need to save receipts for at least that long.

If you file your own taxes, be sure to check and re-check your math. According to the IRS, errors in addition and subtraction are the number one kind of mistake taxpayers make on their returns. All returns are examined for these types of errors. If the mix-up leads to a tax deficiency—meaning that you did not pay enough tax—the IRS will send you a bill for the difference. On the other hand, if it turns out that you have made an error in the government's favor the IRS will either credit you towards future taxes or refund you the extra money.

Once you've calculated all your itemized deductions, you can subtract those from your adjusted gross income. Usually, the remainder will be your taxable income. Depending on your particular situation, you'll be directed to one of several tax tables or schedules to find out how much tax you owe. That, however, is still not the end of the story.

The federal tax code allows for a wide variety of credits, which can be subtracted from the tax you owe. For example, if you've paid taxes to a foreign country, you can take a credit for those. There are also credits given to elderly taxpayers and credits for childcare, to name just a few. The credits that are available are constantly changing, so it's always a good idea to consult a tax professional or to check with the IRS to see what sorts of credits you can take.

After you've completed all the schedules and forms, it's important to remember to sign your return before you mail it. Of course, if your calculations indicate that you owe tax on top of what's been withheld from your paychecks, it's important to attach a check for the correct amount. The IRS strongly advises people not to enclose cash with their return; if you do not have a checking account and need to make a tax payment, you can get a cashier's check or money order from your bank.

With your federal tax return complete, you may be tempted to heave a sigh of relief. Keep in mind, though, that most states impose income tax as well, and that your state tax return is due at the same time as your federal return. The good news is that many states base their income taxes on the federal tax, meaning that much of your work is already done. There's a good chance that all you'll need to do is transfer some numbers from your federal return to appropriate blanks on your state return. For this reason, it's always a good idea to fill out your state tax forms before you seal the envelope containing your federal tax return.

Having submitted your tax returns, you can give yourself a pat on the back. With luck, the only thing you'll get back from the IRS or your state government is a check—if you're due a refund. For a very small percentage of taxpayers, what they get in the mail is far less pleasant: a notice of an audit.

BEWARE OF THE AUDIT

Getting audited ranks up there with root canal therapy on the list of things most people would like to avoid. Many people imagine an IRS audit to involve a stern-faced auditor showing up on the front stoop, demanding to see every receipt and scrap of documentation. Although such "field audits" are occasionally ordered, they are the exception to the rule. Many IRS audits, in fact, are done through the mail. If you are audited, you'll probably be told exactly what deduction is being questioned. This will, at least, make your job of providing documentation less difficult. You'll also be told what documentation is required and how to submit it.

Income tax audits happen for any number of reasons. Most often, you are audited because a business or person with whom you have worked has reported information that doesn't match what you submitted on your tax return. For example, if you report paying more interest on loans than the institutions that made those loans reported, the tax authorities are likely to demand an explanation from you. Of course, if the IRS or your state tax authorities have any reason to believe that you're concealing income or claiming deductions to which you're not entitled, an audit will be done.

If your return was prepared by a tax professional and you receive notice of an audit, be certain that you notify your preparer. Keep in mind, though, that you are the one who signed the tax return. Your tax preparer may explain how the return was prepared but probably will not negotiate with the IRS on your behalf.

If you prepared your own return and have confidence in your ability to explain the questionable areas of your tax return, consider handling the matter yourself. Hiring an accountant or attorney after you've submitted your return and received an audit notice is going to be expensive. Of course, if you have knowingly falsified information on your tax return, you are probably in for a very unpleasant experience. In that case, hiring a qualified attorney is a must.

Whether you bring a tax professional with you or go in on your own, be prepared to justify the deductions that are being questioned. Although there's a good chance that you'll end up owing additional tax, it's worth keeping in mind that the auditor is just as much a human being as you are. This means that he or she will want to be treated courteously and with respect. If you are clear in your presentation of the facts and offer proper documentation, you're likely to be treated with respect in return. If you enter the auditor's office displaying an aggressive or bullying attitude, or if you appear uncertain and confused, you're not likely to be pleased with the result.

Dealing with income taxes is rarely a pleasant experience, but if you pay careful attention and are thorough in your record keeping, you can minimize the financial pain from income taxes.

WORKSHEETS IN THIS CHAPTER:

· **Income Tax Annual Summary Worksheet:** Use this worksheet to record your deductions and withholdings for the year. Refer to these amounts during tax season.

· **Tax-Deductible Expense Worksheet:** Write down your deductible expenses for the year, including interest paid on your mortgage, work expenses, costs of opening a business, relocation expenses, medical expenses, etc.

· **Your Paystub Explained:** This sheet offers a line-by-line explanation of your paystub and the sections that are important for you to pay attention to.

· **Form W-2 Explained:** Each line of the W-2 form in detail, and why this form is important to your tax records.

· **Form W-4 Explained:** A helpful explanation of how to interpret your W-4 form.

INCOME TAX ANNUAL SUMMARY WORKSHEET

Primary Salary/Commissions:

(name of income source/employer)														
	Jan.	Feb.	March	April	May	June	July	Aug.	Sept.	Oct.	Nov.	Dec.	Year Totals	Mo. Avg.
Gross pay (before with-holdings)														
Federal taxes														
State taxes														
Local taxes														
FICA (retirement fund)														
Other deductions														
Net pay (after with-holdings)														

▲
Total Annual Income from Primary Salary
(Sum of all Year Totals)

Secondary Salary/Commissions:

(name of income source/employer)														
	Jan.	Feb.	March	April	May	June	July	Aug.	Sept.	Oct.	Nov.	Dec.	Year Totals	Mo. Avg.
Gross pay (before with-holdings)														
Federal taxes														
State taxes														
Local taxes														
FICA (retirement fund)														
Other deductions														
Net pay (after with-holdings)														

▲
Total Annual Income from Primary Salary
(Sum of all Year Totals)

Type:

Date	Description	Amount
/		$
/		$
/		$
/		$
/		$
/		$
/		$
/		$
/		$
/		$
/		$
/		$
/		$

Type:

Date	Description	Amount
/		$
/		$
/		$
/		$
/		$
/		$
/		$
/		$
/		$
/		$
/		$
/		$
/		$

Type:

Date	Description	Amount
/		$
/		$
/		$
/		$
/		$
/		$
/		$
/		$
/		$
/		$
/		$
/		$

Type:

Date	Description	Amount
/		$
/		$
/		$
/		$
/		$
/		$
/		$
/		$
/		$
/		$
/		$
/		$

Speedy Shipping Company
14362 Sunnyville Drive
San Diego, CA 92143-6292

Employee Paystub   Check Number: Pay Period: 07/12/2009-07/25/2009   Pay Date: 07/27/2009

Employee			SSN	Status (Fed/State)	Allowances/Extra
Jane Doe, 16020 Blank Road, San Diego, CA 92313			***-**-1034	Single/Single	Fed-2/0/CA-2/0

Earnings & Hours	Qty	Rate	Current	YTD Amount
Salary			1,923.08	28,726.01
Sick Salary				37.02
Vacation Salary				83.17
Overtime Hrly.				673.12
Total			1,923.08	29,519.32

Direct Deposit	Amount
Checking - ******0000	1,392.33

Paid Time Off	YTD Used	Available
Sick	1.54	21.56
Vacation	3.46	54.38

Deductions From Gross	Current	YTD Amount
Simple IRA - Employee	-57.69	-865.35

Non-taxable Items	Current	YTD Amount
Simple IRA - Co.	57.69	885.55

Taxes	Current	YTD Amount
Federal Withholding	-242.00	-3,799.00
Social Security Employee	-119.23	-1,830.20
Medicare Employee	-27.88	-428.03
CA - Withholding	-72.41	-1,148.76
CA - Disability Employee	-11.54	-177.12
Total	-473.06	-7,383.11

Adjustments to Net Pay	Current	YTD Amount
Office Expense Reimbursement		25.00

Net Pay		
	1,392.33	21,295.86

1. Name and address of employer

2. This line includes the check number (unless directly deposited), the pay start and end dates, and pay date information.

3. This area lists your name, address, Social Security Number, and tax filing status (marital status and allowances).

4. Your current and year-to-date earnings are listed here.

5. If you use direct deposit the account type and routing number will be shown with the net amount deposited.

6. Shows current sick and vacation time available and the year-to-date sick and vacation time used.

7. Lists any deductions subtracted from your gross pay before taxes are calculated.

8. Lists the current and year-to-date non-taxable items from your gross pay.

9. Lists any deductions subtracted from your gross pay after taxes are calculated.

10. Lists any after tax adjustments to net pay.

11. Shows the total current and year-to-date "take-home" portion of your paycheck.

This is a sample IRS Form W-2

<table>
<tr><td colspan="2"></td><td>a Employee's social security number</td><td colspan="2">OMB No. 1545-0008</td><td colspan="2">Safe, accurate,
FAST! Use IRS e-file</td><td>Visit the IRS website
at www.irs.gov/efile.</td></tr>
<tr><td colspan="2">b Employer identification number (EIN)</td><td></td><td></td><td colspan="2">1 Wages, tips, other compensation</td><td colspan="2">2 Federal income tax withheld</td></tr>
<tr><td colspan="3">c Employer's name, address, and ZIP code</td><td></td><td colspan="2">3 Social security wages</td><td colspan="2">4 Social security tax withheld</td></tr>
<tr><td colspan="3"></td><td></td><td colspan="2">5 Medicare wages and tips</td><td colspan="2">6 Medicare tax withheld</td></tr>
<tr><td colspan="3"></td><td></td><td colspan="2">7 Social security tips</td><td colspan="2">8 Allocated tips</td></tr>
<tr><td colspan="3">d Control number</td><td></td><td colspan="2">9 Advance EIC payment</td><td colspan="2">10 Dependent care benefits</td></tr>
<tr><td colspan="3">e Employee's first name and initial   Last name   Suff.</td><td></td><td colspan="2">11 Nonqualified plans</td><td colspan="2">12a See instructions for box 12</td></tr>
<tr><td colspan="3"></td><td></td><td colspan="2">13 Statutory employee / Retirement plan / Third-party sick pay</td><td colspan="2">12b</td></tr>
<tr><td colspan="3"></td><td></td><td colspan="2">14 Other</td><td colspan="2">12c</td></tr>
<tr><td colspan="3"></td><td></td><td colspan="2"></td><td colspan="2">12d</td></tr>
<tr><td colspan="3">f Employee's address and ZIP code</td><td></td><td colspan="2"></td><td colspan="2"></td></tr>
<tr><td>15 State   Employer's state ID number</td><td colspan="2">16 State wages, tips, etc.</td><td>17 State income tax</td><td colspan="2">18 Local wages, tips, etc.</td><td>19 Local income tax</td><td>20 Locality name</td></tr>
</table>

Form **W-2** Wage and Tax Statement   **2007**   Department of the Treasury—Internal Revenue Service

Copy B—To Be Filed With Employee's FEDERAL Tax Return.
This information is being furnished to the Internal Revenue Service.

YOUR W-2 FORM

At the end of the year, every employer you worked for should send you a Form W-2. You'll need at least some of the information on each W-2 in order to fill out your federal, state, and local tax returns. There should be multiple copies of each W-2. You'll need to attach these copies to the returns you file.

INTERPRETING YOUR W-2

Whether or not you need all the information on your
W-2 depends on your individual situation. However, by understanding what the numbers in each box mean, you'll know what (if anything) to do with the information, and be able to check your W-2 for accuracy.

Box a - This should have your social security number (SSN) in it. Be certain it's correct; if this number doesn't match the number on your tax return, the IRS will probably consider your tax return incomplete.

Box b - This number is used by the IRS to match the information on the W-2 with other reports your employer has filed with the government. You don't need to put this number on your tax return, though.

Box c - This is just information the IRS uses if it needs to contact your employer. Make sure it's correct; if it isn't, make the necessary changes on all three copies of your W-2.

FORM W-2 EXPLAINED

Box d - The IRS doesn't require your employer to fill in this box, which is for the Control Number. If the box is blank, there's no need for concern.

Box e - This is self-explanatory. Just make sure your name is correctly spelled. Make corrections on all copies of the W-2, if necessary.

Box f - This is also self-explanatory. Correct your address if necessary.

Box 1 - This box should list the dollar amount of all your taxable income. The figure may be higher than what you received as salary, since it includes tips, taxable fringe benefits, and bonuses. If the W-2 is from a former employer, this box may also include things like severance pay and vacation pay, which is also taxable.

Box 2 - This box shows how much federal tax your employer withheld from your pay during the year. You'll need to list this on the appropriate line in your tax return.

Box 3 - This box shows the portion of your pay that was subject to social security tax. Because some earnings are not subject to social security tax, this figure may be different from the one shown in Box 1.

Box 4 - This box shows how much social security tax your employer withheld. If you had more than one employer, there's a chance that too much social security tax was withheld. In that case, read the instructions for your tax return to see if you qualify for a refund of some of this tax.

Box 5 - This box shows how much of your income was subject to Medicare tax. This figure may or may not match the figures in Box 1 or Box 3.

Box 6 - This box shows how much Medicare tax your employer withheld.

Box 7 - If you reported tips to your employer, the total amount will be shown here. This figure is part of the total shown in Box 1.

Box 8 - If you worked for a restaurant, this box shows the difference between the tips you reported to your employer and your share of a percentage of the restaurant's income. Usually, that's your share of 8 percent of the restaurant's income. The amount shown in this box isn't included in the figure in Box 1, so you'll need to add Box 8's amount to Box 1's when you fill out your tax return. You may also need to pay social security tax and Medicare tax on the amount shown in Box 8; the instructions that came with your tax return will tell you how to go about doing this.

Box 9 - This box indicates your Advance Earned Income payment. If you received an Advance Earned Income Credit, this amount will be deducted from the credit you claim on your tax return.

Box 10 - This box shows any reimbursements you received from your employer for money you spent on day-care for a dependent. This amount may already have been included in the amount shown in Box 1. If there's anything shown in Box 10, you'll need to fill out Form 2441, Child and Dependent Care Expenses, to see if you owe any additional tax.

Box 11 - This box shows money you received from certain retirement or deferred compensation plans. Depending on the source of the money shown here, the amount will already be included in the figure shown in Box 1, Box 3, or Box 5.

Box 12 - This box will show a dollar figure followed by a letter-code that indicates the source of the money. Depending on which code is shown, you may have to report the income shown.

Box 13 - One of the small boxes here may be checked. Checks in one or more of these boxes may affect how you can deduct business expenses and retirement plan contributions, and/or whether you have to pay tax on sick pay.

Box 14 - This box will show amounts that were withheld from your pay for such things as union dues, premiums for health insurance, or amounts paid toward school tuition. Usually, any figure shown in this box will not be subject to tax, but if you have any questions, you can ask your employer's payroll department for advice.

Boxes 15-20 - The information shown in these boxes will be used in filing your state and local tax returns, if any. Usually, you will use amounts shown in your federal tax return when you fill out your state and local returns. However, if you itemize your deductions on your federal return, you'll need to list the figures in boxes 17 and 20, since these show how much state and local tax you paid.

Box 15 - Employer's state and I.D. number

Box 16 - Your state wages, tips and other taxable income

Box 17 - Total state income tax that was withheld from your pay

Box 18 - Locality name

Box 19 - Your local wages, tips and other taxable income

Box 20 - Total local income tax that was withheld from your pay

This is a sample IRS Form W-4

Form W-4 (2007)

Purpose. Complete Form W-4 so that your employer can withhold the correct federal income tax from your pay. Because your tax situation may change, you may want to refigure your withholding each year.

Exemption from withholding. If you are exempt, complete **only** lines 1, 2, 3, 4, and 7 and sign the form to validate it. Your exemption for 2007 expires February 16, 2008. See Pub. 505, Tax Withholding and Estimated Tax.

Note. You cannot claim exemption from withholding if (a) your income exceeds $850 and includes more than $300 of unearned income (for example, interest and dividends) and (b) another person can claim you as a dependent on their tax return.

Basic instructions. If you are not exempt, complete the **Personal Allowances Worksheet** below. The worksheets on page 2 adjust your withholding allowances based on itemized deductions, certain credits, adjustments to income, or two-earner/multiple job situations. Complete all worksheets that apply. However, you may claim fewer (or zero) allowances.

Head of household. Generally, you may claim head of household filing status on your tax return only if you are unmarried and pay more than 50% of the costs of keeping up a home for yourself and your dependent(s) or other qualifying individuals.

Tax credits. You can take projected tax credits into account in figuring your allowable number of withholding allowances. Credits for child or dependent care expenses and the child tax credit may be claimed using the **Personal Allowances Worksheet** below. See Pub. 919, How Do I Adjust My Tax Withholding, for information on converting your other credits into withholding allowances.

Nonwage income. If you have a large amount of nonwage income, such as interest or dividends, consider making estimated tax payments using Form 1040-ES, Estimated Tax for Individuals. Otherwise, you may owe additional tax. If you have pension or annuity income, see Pub. 919 to find out if you should adjust your withholding on Form W-4 or W-4P.

Two earners/Multiple jobs. If you have a working spouse or more than one job, figure the total number of allowances you are entitled to claim on all jobs using worksheets from only one Form W-4. Your withholding usually will be most accurate when all allowances are claimed on the Form W-4 for the highest paying job and zero allowances are claimed on the others.

Nonresident alien. If you are a nonresident alien, see the Instructions for Form 8233 before completing this Form W-4.

Check your withholding. After your Form W-4 takes effect, use Pub. 919 to see how the dollar amount you are having withheld compares to your projected total tax for 2007. See Pub. 919, especially if your earnings exceed $130,000 (Single) or $180,000 (Married).

Personal Allowances Worksheet (Keep for your records.)

A Enter "1" for **yourself** if no one else can claim you as a dependent . . . . **A** _____

B Enter "1" if:
- You are single and have only one job; or
- You are married, have only one job, and your spouse does not work; or
- Your wages from a second job or your spouse's wages (or the total of both) are $1,000 or less.

. . **B** _____

C Enter "1" for your **spouse.** But, you may choose to enter "-0-" if you are married and have either a working spouse or more than one job. (Entering "-0-" may help you avoid having too little tax withheld.) . . . . **C** _____

D Enter number of **dependents** (other than your spouse or yourself) you will claim on your tax return . . . . . . **D** _____

E Enter "1" if you will file as **head of household** on your tax return (see conditions under **Head of household** above) . **E** _____

F Enter "1" if you have at least $1,500 of **child or dependent care expenses** for which you plan to claim a credit . . **F** _____
(Note. Do not include child support payments. See Pub. 503, Child and Dependent Care Expenses, for details.)

G **Child Tax Credit** (including additional child tax credit). See Pub 972, Child Tax Credit, for more information.
- If your total income will be less than $57,000 ($85,000 if married), enter "2" for each eligible child.
- If your total income will be between $57,000 and $84,000 ($85,000 and $119,000 if married), enter "1" for each eligible child plus "1" additional if you have 4 or more eligible children. . . . . . . **G** _____

H Add lines A through G and enter total here. (Note. This may be different from the number of exemptions you claim on your tax return.) ▶ **H** _____

For accuracy, complete all worksheets that apply.
- If you plan to **itemize or claim adjustments** to income and want to reduce your withholding, see the **Deductions and Adjustments Worksheet** on page 2.
- If you have **more than one job** or are **married and you and your spouse both work** and the combined earnings from all jobs exceed $40,000 ($25,000 if married) see the **Two-Earners/Multiple Jobs Worksheet** on page 2 to avoid having too little tax withheld.
- If **neither** of the above situations applies, stop here and enter the number from line H on line 5 of Form W-4 below.

- - - - - - - - - - - - - - - - - - - Cut here and give Form W-4 to your employer. Keep the top part for your records. - - - - - - - - - - - -

Form **W-4**	**Employee's Withholding Allowance Certificate**	OMB No. 1545-0074
Department of the Treasury Internal Revenue Service	▶ Whether you are entitled to claim a certain number of allowances or exemption from withholding is subject to review by the IRS. Your employer may be required to send a copy of this form to the IRS.	2007

1	Type or print your first name and middle initial	Last name		2	Your social security number

Home address (number and street or rural route)		3 ☐ Single ☐ Married ☐ Married, but withhold at higher Single rate. Note. If married, but legally separated, or spouse is a nonresident alien, check the "Single" box.
City or town, state, and ZIP code		4 If your last name differs from that shown on your social security card, check here. You must call 1-800-772-1213 for a replacement card. ▶ ☐

5	Total number of allowances you are claiming (from line **H** above or from the applicable worksheet on page 2)	**5**
6	Additional amount, if any, you want withheld from each paycheck	**6** $
7	I claim exemption from withholding for 2007, and I certify that I meet **both** of the following conditions for exemption.
	• Last year I had a right to a refund of **all** federal income tax withheld because I had **no** tax liability **and**
	• This year I expect a refund of **all** federal income tax withheld because I expect to have **no** tax liability.
	If you meet both conditions, write "Exempt" here . . . . ▶ **7**

Under penalties of perjury, I declare that I have examined this certificate and to the best of my knowledge and belief, it is true, correct, and complete.

Employee's signature
(Form is not valid unless you sign it.) ▶ _____ Date ▶ _____

8	Employer's name and address (Employer: Complete lines 8 and 10 only if sending to the IRS.)	9 Office code (optional)	10 Employer identification number (EIN)

For Privacy Act and Paperwork Reduction Act Notice, see page 2.   Cat. No. 10220Q   Form **W-4** (2007)

Form W-4 (2007) — Page **2**

Deductions and Adjustments Worksheet

Note. Use this worksheet *only* if you plan to itemize deductions, claim certain credits, or claim adjustments to income on your 2007 tax return.

1. Enter an estimate of your 2007 itemized deductions. These include qualifying home mortgage interest, charitable contributions, state and local taxes, medical expenses in excess of 7.5% of your income, and miscellaneous deductions. (For 2007, you may have to reduce your itemized deductions if your income is over $156,400 ($78,200 if married filing separately). See *Worksheet 2* in Pub. 919 for details.) . . **1** $ _____

2. Enter: { $10,700 if married filing jointly or qualifying widow(er) / $ 7,850 if head of household / $ 5,350 if single or married filing separately } . . . . . **2** $ _____

3. Subtract line 2 from line 1. If zero or less, enter "-0-" . . . . **3** $ _____
4. Enter an estimate of your 2007 adjustments to income, including alimony, deductible IRA contributions, and student loan interest **4** $ _____
5. Add lines 3 and 4 and enter the total. (Include any amount for credits from *Worksheet 8* in Pub. 919) . **5** $ _____
6. Enter an estimate of your 2007 nonwage income (such as dividends or interest) . . . . **6** $ _____
7. Subtract line 6 from line 5. If zero or less, enter "-0-" . . . . **7** $ _____
8. Divide the amount on line 7 by $3,400 and enter the result here. Drop any fraction . . . **8** _____
9. Enter the number from the **Personal Allowances Worksheet**, line H, page 1 . . . . . . **9** _____
10. Add lines 8 and 9 and enter the total here. If you plan to use the **Two-Earners/Multiple Jobs Worksheet**, also enter this total on line 1 below. Otherwise, stop here and enter this total on Form W-4, line 5, page 1 **10** _____

Two-Earners/Multiple Jobs Worksheet (See *Two earners/multiple jobs* on page 1.)

Note. Use this worksheet *only* if the instructions under line H on page 1 direct you here.

1. Enter the number from line H, page 1 (or from line 10 above if you used the **Deductions and Adjustments Worksheet**) **1** _____
2. Find the number in **Table 1** below that applies to the **LOWEST** paying job and enter it here. However, if you are married filing jointly and wages from the highest paying job are $50,000 or less, do not enter more than "3." . . . . **2** _____
3. If line 1 is more than or equal to line 2, subtract line 2 from line 1. Enter the result here (if zero, enter "-0-") and on Form W-4, line 5, page 1. **Do not use the rest of this worksheet** . . . . . . **3** _____

Note. If line 1 is *less than* line 2, enter "-0-" on Form W-4, line 5, page 1. Complete lines 4–9 below to calculate the additional withholding amount necessary to avoid a year-end tax bill.

4. Enter the number from line 2 of this worksheet . . . . **4** _____
5. Enter the number from line 1 of this worksheet . . . . **5** _____
6. Subtract line 5 from line 4 . . . . **6** _____
7. Find the amount in Table 2 below that applies to the **HIGHEST** paying job and enter it here . . . . **7** $ _____
8. Multiply line 7 by line 6 and enter the result here. This is the additional annual withholding needed . . **8** $ _____
9. Divide line 8 by the number of pay periods remaining in 2007. For example, divide by 26 if you are paid every two weeks and you complete this form in December 2006. Enter the result here and on Form W-4, line 6, page 1. This is the additional amount to be withheld from each paycheck . . . . **9** $ _____

Table 1				Table 2			
Married Filing Jointly		**All Others**		**Married Filing Jointly**		**All Others**	
If wages from LOWEST paying job are—	Enter on line 2 above	If wages from LOWEST paying job are—	Enter on line 2 above	If wages from HIGHEST paying job are—	Enter on line 7 above	If wages from HIGHEST paying job are—	Enter on line 7 above
$0 - $4,500	0	$0 - $6,000	0	$0 - $65,000	$510	$0 - $35,000	$510
4,501 - 9,000	1	6,001 - 12,000	1	65,001 - 120,000	850	35,001 - 80,000	850
9,001 - 18,000	2	12,001 - 19,000	2	120,001 - 170,000	950	80,001 - 150,000	950
18,001 - 22,000	3	19,001 - 26,000	3	170,001 - 300,000	1,120	150,001 - 340,000	1,120
22,001 - 26,000	4	26,001 - 35,000	4	300,001 and over	1,190	340,001 and over	1,190
26,001 - 32,000	5	35,001 - 50,000	5				
32,001 - 38,000	6	50,001 - 65,000	6				
38,001 - 46,000	7	65,001 - 80,000	7				
46,001 - 55,000	8	80,001 - 90,000	8				
55,001 - 60,000	9	90,001 - 120,000	9				
60,001 - 65,000	10	120,001 and over	10				
65,001 - 75,000	11						
75,001 - 95,000	12						
95,001 - 105,000	13						
105,001 - 120,000	14						
120,001 and over	15						

FORM W-4: EMPLOYEE'S WITHHOLDING ALLOWANCE CERTIFICATE

On the first day at a new job, your employer will ask you to fill out a W-4 form. Your answers to the questions on this form will be used to determine how much of your pay will be withheld for federal, state, and local income taxes. Fill out the worksheets that come with the form, using your best estimates of things like deductions and adjustments to your income. Then complete and sign the W-4 itself. If you find later on that your income or deductions will be substantially different from what you estimated, you can file a new W-4 with your employer.

Form W-4 itself is very simple. Here is what you'll be asked to provide:

1) Your name and address

2) Your social security number

3) Your marital status. Be sure to check the "single" box if you're married to a non-resident alien.

4) Check this box if the name you show on this form is different from the one on your social security card.

5) The number of allowances you're claiming. This number will have been calculated using one or more of the worksheets that come with Form W-4.

6) Additional amount you want withheld. Some people prefer to have extra money withheld so that they don't have to pay additional tax when they file their return. (Remember, though, that if you have more money withheld than you'll actually owe, you're giving the government an interest-free loan!)

7) If you meet the conditions shown here, write "Exempt" in this blank.

8-10) This information will be filled in by your employer.

INSURANCE

Any plan for building wealth must include protecting yourself against the sudden loss of your assets. Natural disasters like storms or fires can destroy property. A serious illness or injury can keep you from working and lead to ruinously high medical bills. And should you die unexpectedly, those who depend on you will suddenly face a dramatic loss of income. Although insurance is something you hope you'll never need, it is invaluable for helping you or your loved ones recover from disasters like these.

Insurance tends to be one of the most widely purchased but least understood financial products around. Although many Americans carry insurance, experts say that 90 percent of them either carry the wrong type or the wrong amount. Learning how much and what kind of insurance you need is one of the most important steps you can take to protect your assets. After all, it does little good to put time and effort into building wealth if you leave it unprotected.

The proper amount of insurance can take the sting out of events that would otherwise be financial catastrophes. For example, health insurance can cover what could be astronomical medical bills when someone has an accident or falls ill and needs to be hospitalized. Similarly, long-term disability insurance helps protect earnings in the event that an injury or chronic illness leaves you unable to work. And in the event of your death, life insurance can provide financial support for the people who depend on your income.

There are some important terms you should familiarize yourself with before buying insurance. The first of these terms is coverage. Simply put, coverage is the amount of money a policy will pay out on the insured. For example if you buy a life insurance policy with $50,000 worth of coverage, the insurance company will pay that amount to whoever you name as the beneficiary when you die.

Another important term is premium, which is the amount of money you pay for a specific amount of coverage. Premiums are usually based on the insurance company's calculations of the risk that it will have to pay a claim. When insurance companies consider whether to insure you, they assess what level of risk you pose to them. For example, if you're in your 20s, you will pay less for a life insurance policy than you will if you're in your 50s. This is because the probability of a healthy 20-something dying is much lower than that of a 50-something dying.

Insurance companies place potential customers in one of four risk groups: preferred, standard, substandard, and uninsurable. Preferred customers are offered the lowest premiums because they pose the lowest risk. Standard customers will pay higher premiums because they represent an increased risk over preferred customers. Substandard customers are viewed as even more risky than standard customers. Finally, people who fall into the uninsurable category are considered to be too risky to insure at all.

The policy's deductible is the amount of money the insurance company holds back when it pays on a claim. Most insurance policies have some kind of deductible, although it's not always called that. For example, companies that offer disability insurance usually state in their policies that there's a waiting period before payments begin. That waiting period, whatever its length, amounts to money that the company isn't paying out. It is important to note that deductibles and premiums have an inverse relationship: The higher your deductible is, the lower your premium will be, since higher deductibles reduce the amount the insurance company pays on each claim.

There are numerous types of insurance, each of which can protect you from different kinds of losses.

LIFE INSURANCE

In its simplest form, life insurance pays benefits to the person you name as your beneficiary in the event of your death. Life insurance is an excellent way to see that your dependants are cared for in the event of your death; it can pay for a child's education, help pay off debts, or pay for your loved ones' living expenses (at least for a time).

When you go shopping for life insurance, you'll quickly find yourself facing a wide array of choices. The first thing to decide is what type of insurance policy will meet your needs. There are two basic types of policies: cash value policies and term policies. Cash value policies provide protection for your dependants and build up a cash balance over the years that you can use later on. If you decide to surrender the policy, the accumulated cash value will be returned to you. You also have the option of borrowing against the cash value of the policy. If you die before the loan is repaid, the outstanding balance of the loan will be deducted from the insurance benefit. A cash value policy stays in effect for as long as you own it, and the premiums usually are fixed.

Unlike cash value policies, term policies provide coverage for a specified length of time, or term. The premium you pay buys insurance for the specified term. Once you stop paying premiums, the coverage lapses. Although premiums tend to be very low when you're young, they increase as you get older. This type of policy does not allow for the build-up of any cash value.

Although most Americans are covered by some type of life insurance, not everyone needs life insurance. For example, if you are single and have no debts or dependents, you probably do not even need life insurance. Likewise, if you are wealthy and know that your loved ones will be amply provided for in the event of your death, you probably do not need life insurance. Working couples who have no debts and who would not be financially affected by the loss of one partner generally do not need life insurance either. Also, there is generally no need for parents to carry insurance on their children's lives.

Even though some people don't need insurance, there are plenty of others who should have at least some life insurance. For example, let's say you are married and your spouse is dependent on your income. In the event of your death, life insurance would provide at least some support for your spouse until he or she can begin working. Another situation that calls for life insurance is if you have dependent children.

If you decide you do need life insurance, you have to determine the right amount of coverage. If you have debts, it makes sense to buy enough coverage to pay those off so that your loved ones don't have to. Some people, even if they have no debts, buy a small amount of insurance to pay for any funeral expenses. If you have dependent children, you probably need more coverage. Your policy should be written not only to cover major debts and funeral expenses but should include enough money to provide for their living expenses and the cost of their college education. There are websites, such as one provided by T. Rowe Price (www.troweprice.com), that can help you estimate how much your children might need to pay for college.

If you have a non-working spouse, or if you earn a lot more than your spouse does, you may want to consider buying coverage equal to the amount of your income over the years remaining until your retirement. For example, if you make $40,000 per year and you have 10 years left until retirement, you should consider buying coverage of at least $400,000. Such an amount might seem high to some and low to others. It's important to give careful thought to your particular situation before buying life insurance.

Although it is often necessary, life insurance is considered by many leaders in the financial industry to be the most oversold of all financial products. These experts say that cash value policies are especially oversold. The reason for this, many say, is that sales people earn commissions on cash value policies that are 8 to 10 times higher than commissions on term policies. Thus, there is a huge incentive for insurance sales people to promote cash value policies. What often makes cash value policies a poor option is that in many cases the commissions are built directly into the premium; this means that for the first year or two the cash value does not build up at all.

Your insurance agent might try to sell you a cash value policy by pointing out that premiums on this policy will stay the same as you age. However, keep in mind that life insurance is not necessarily something you will need for your entire life. Life insurance is most often bought when a person is younger and has a number of substantial financial commitments. As you get older, your financial obligations should lessen—your children will no longer be dependent on you, and you may not have as much debt as you had when you were younger. You might, therefore, find that you can save money by purchasing a term policy with lower coverage. And even though cash value policies build up a cash balance, you can achieve the same result by having money deducted from your paycheck and deposited into an IRA or 401(k). Better yet, you don't have to pay someone a sales commission to do so.

Insurance agents often make much of the fact that you can borrow money against your policy, and this is true enough. The problem with this is that the insurance company will charge you interest for that loan. In effect, you end up paying interest for borrowing money that was yours to begin with! These issues are worth considering before committing to a cash value policy.

Term insurance policies, of course, have drawbacks of their own. First, term insurance gets more expensive as your age and your likelihood of dying increases. Insurance companies sometimes offer the option of locking in the same premium for 10 or 15 years, even though the term of the policy remains the same. Whether or not the peace of mind that stability gives you is worth the higher overall cost of the insurance is something you have to decide for yourself. Additionally, because some insurance policies require periodic medical exams in order to maintain eligibility for lower rates, you may decide that avoiding the inconvenience of a physical exam justifies the extra expense.

A second consideration is whether or not the policy is guaranteed to be renewable. Better policies offer this feature. It means the company can't refuse to renew your policy if your health declines. Unless you expect to let the policy lapse once the term ends, this is can be a valuable feature.

No matter what kind of insurance you buy, you'll find that being able to show that you're in good health will save you money. Insurance companies go to great lengths to estimate the life expectancy of each customer. If your lifestyle, physical condition, or occupation put you at risk of dying young, you will have to pay more to get the same coverage that someone else who is less at risk of dying gets. Simply put, the lower the probability that an insurance company will have to pay a death benefit, the less it will charge for the policy.

Insurance companies charge extra for policies that are "guaranteed issue," meaning that they do not require you to have a physical exam before they insure you. Unless you believe that you have a physical condition that could shorten your life, it makes sense to submit to the exam. Even though the physical exam may take a little time and require a visit to a doctor chosen by the company, the minor inconvenience will probably save you money.

You can also save money by adopting a healthier lifestyle. If you smoke, quit: Smokers pay higher rates than non-smokers. If you're overweight, make an effort to lose those extra pounds. People who are overweight are charged extra because they're at risk of dying prematurely. Not only will embracing a healthy lifestyle save you money but it will also pay off in terms of feeling better!

HEALTH / DENTAL INSURANCE

Health insurance covers a portion of your medical expenses when you are sick or injured. Coverage can vary, depending on the circumstances under which the expenses are incurred. For example, some health insurance policies cover hospital charges only if you stay overnight. A visit to your doctor's office may be covered almost completely, while a visit to a doctor in a hospital's emergency room requires you to pay a greater share of the fee. When it comes to health insurance, the kinds and amounts of coverage you can get are virtually endless.

No matter what sort of coverage you buy, most health and dental insurance policies require you to pay at least a small portion of the doctor's or the dentist's fee. This is what is known as the co-payment. In addition to specifying a co-payment, many policies require that the insured must pay a deductible. This is a set amount of money the insured pays out-of-pocket before the insurance company makes any payments. Deductibles are often imposed each year, meaning that even if you pay the deductible this year, you'll have to pay it again next year, and so on.

The price of medical care in the United States is so expensive that pretty much everyone—even very wealthy people—buys health insurance. Just one overnight hospital stay, for example, can cost thousands of dollars, depending on what illness or injury sent you there. Even more financially catastrophic can be treatment for chronic conditions such as diabetes, which can cost more than $100,000 a year. Having health insurance, therefore, is a valuable safety net and can prevent you from being bankrupted by medical bills.

Since the 1980s, much of the emphasis in the health insurance industry has been on managed care. The term managed care describes a policy that emphasizes having one healthcare provider who keeps track of the policyholder's care. The goal of managed care is to encourage people to see their doctor regularly and prevent illness, instead of waiting until a serious illness requiring expensive treatment develops.

The three most common types of managed-care plans offered by insurance companies are Health Maintenance Organizations (HMOs), Exclusive Provider Organizations (EPOs), and Preferred Provider Organizations (PPOs).

An HMO offers access to a group of doctors, nurses, and other medical professionals known as a network. The insured person is required to choose a doctor who serves as the primary care physician (also referred to as a PCP). If you need to see a specialist, your PCP must first authorize a referral. In HMOs, all medical services need to be obtained from a provider within the network. Visits to doctors who aren't part of the network are not covered. HMOs charge a flat monthly rate for insurance, and although there are no deductibles, the insured will typically have to pay a small co-pay for each office visit.

An EPO is similar to an HMO in that it offers care through a network of providers. The insured is not always required to have a primary care physician, however. In this case, the insured is allowed to "self-refer," or visit any doctor or specialist within the network.

INSURANCE

Like the other types of managed-care plans, a PPO encourages its customers to obtain care from a network of doctors and specialists. However, PPOs do not limit the insured to a single network. Should you want to see someone outside the network, you are free to do so. The PPO will still pay most of the expenses, although out-of-network visits will likely cost you a higher co-pay than in-network visits cost. If you see a doctor outside of the network, you will also probably have to pay a deductible.

Another difference between PPOs, HMOs, and EPOs is the way each bills for its services. HMOs and EPOs pay healthcare providers directly. PPOs, on the other hand, require you to pay the medical expenses out-of-pocket. The invoice is then sent to the insurance company for reimbursement. Depending on your own situation, you may feel that the increased flexibility offered by a PPO is worth the added expense and inconvenience.

The premiums charged by health insurers can be hundreds of dollars per month. Fortunately, many people with full-time jobs receive health insurance through their employers. Large corporations, especially, are able to offer their employees good health insurance at a relatively low cost because they get a discount from their insurance company. Although the employer may not pay the entire cost of the premiums, the cost to employees is significantly less than they would pay if they were to purchase a policy on their own. Even if you're self-employed, you might be able to get at least a small discount on health insurance premiums by banding together with other self-employed individuals or groups of small businesses.

No matter how you purchase health insurance, your personal health history will determine the type of coverage you are eligible to receive. When you apply for health coverage, the company will ask if you have current medical problems (what are known as "pre-existing conditions"). Some insurance companies will charge extra for your insurance and may even decline to sell you insurance at all if you appear to be a high-risk customer.

At least some of your health history ends up on file with an organization known as the Medical Information Bureau (MIB). If you have been turned down for insurance, you can write to the Medical Information Bureau at P.O. Box 105, Essex Station, Boston MA, 02112, or visit their website at www.mib.com to request a copy of your file. Should you find a mistake, you can request that it be fixed, but you will have to be prepared to prove the information MIB has is incorrect.

Having health insurance is extremely important. Unfortunately, most people eventually face losing their health insurance. For example, if you lose your job, the health insurance you get through your employer will be terminated. Many employers will at least continue coverage for former employees until the end of their last month on the job. So, for example, if your last day of work was the middle of the month, your employer might be willing to continue paying for your coverage through the end of that month.
Although employers all set their own policies about how long to pay for their former employees' insurance, the Consolidated Omnibus Budget Reconciliation Act of 1985, more commonly known as

COBRA, requires most employers to offer former employees the opportunity to continue their coverage at the group rate for up to 18 months. Although you pay the premiums out of your own pocket, you get coverage for the same price your former employer is paying.

MEDICARE

Persons older than 65 are eligible for coverage through the federal government plan known as Medicare. People eligible for Medicare typically receive health insurance for a very modest monthly premium. This is because they pre-paid for part of this benefit with the Medicare taxes that were withheld from their paychecks when they were employed.

Medicare has several parts, the first of which is Hospital Insurance. This portion of Medicare (usually referred to as Part A) pays for such things as hospital stays (including medical tests, meals, and supplies) and rehabilitation. Part A also covers certain medical equipment (wheelchairs, walkers, etc), and hospice care for the terminally ill.

The second part of Medicare (also called Part B) is similar to regular health insurance. For a monthly premium, persons enrolled in this program are covered for doctor's visits. The original Medicare plan, though, is not an HMO, so preventive care in the form of routine check-ups is not included. Long-term care, routine eye care, eyeglasses, dental work, and hearing exams are also not covered. Part B does cover diagnostic tests, outpatient medical services, and home health care. In addition to paying a premium for Part B, retirees are also required to pay an annual deductible before benefits kick in. People who qualify for Medicare can purchase what is called a Medicare Advantage Plan, which is a form of managed care.

Medicare now also offers prescription drug coverage. There are several plans available that vary in cost, depending on deductibles, co-pay, and what state you live in. For more information on the Medicare Prescription Drug plan, go to www.medicare.gov.

Receiving Medicare coverage is pretty straightforward. Part A coverage is automatic, whereas Part B is elective, meaning that someone must actively enroll in the program. Although you are not required to enroll in Part B, there are penalties for not doing so fairly soon after you're eligible. These penalties come in the form of a surcharge of 10 percent of your premium for every year you were eligible but didn't sign up.

In addition to Medicare, some people opt to also enroll in the supplemental insurance program known as Medigap, which, as the name implies, fills in some of the "gaps" that Medicare does not cover. In most cases, those who are enrolled in Medicare Advantage Plans do not need Medigap coverage.

MEDICAID

If you are under the age of 65 and are under- or unemployed, you and members of your family may be eligible for a state-administered insurance program called Medicaid. Medicaid eligibility requirements are very specific and vary from state to state. These requirements include (but may not be limited to) income, age, and whether you are disabled or pregnant.

If a family is ineligible for Medicaid benefits based on income, they may still qualify to receive State Children's Health Insurance Program (SCHIP). SCHIP pays for doctor visits, emergency room visits, hospitalizations, and immunizations for children under the age of 19. To be eligible for SCHIP, a family's annual income must be below a certain level. SCHIP is free or very inexpensive to families who are eligible.

If your employer doesn't offer health insurance as a fringe benefit or requires that you pay part of the premiums, there are ways to keep the cost of your coverage to a minimum. For example, if your employer offers an HMO as one of your insurance options, such a plan will probably give you the most coverage for the least amount of money out of your pocket.

On the other hand, if you're paying for health insurance on your own, another way to save money is to agree to a relatively high co-pay. Typical co-pays range between 10 and 20 percent of the total bill. You can save money on your monthly premium if you decide to go with a plan that calls for you to pay 40 percent of the bill, and even more if you opt for a plan that requires you to pay as much as 80 percent. Obviously, such plans are only appropriate if you are confident that your healthcare needs are going to be modest and that you have the resources to cover the higher co-pays.

You may also want to consider paying out-of-pocket for routine medical and dental visits, opting to only purchase catastrophic coverage. This type of health insurance only covers major medical expenses such as hospital stays, intensive care, diagnostic tests, X-rays, lab tests, and surgery. Because these kinds of medical services can range upwards of $100,000, purchasing catastrophic coverage could potentially save you thousands of dollars in premiums but still protect you from bankruptcy should you experience a major medical problem.

DISABILITY INSURANCE

Disability insurance protects you in the event you become disabled and are unable to work. Many people, especially those whose jobs don't put them at risk of injury, dismiss the need to purchase disability insurance; they believe that their chances of becoming disabled are remote. However, according to the Health Insurance Association of America, persons between the ages of 35 and 65 have as great a chance of becoming disabled as they do of dying. Insurance experts say that unless you are so wealthy that you do not need to work for a living, long-term disability insurance is something you should consider having.

Most long-term disability insurance policies insure you for no more than 60 percent of your salary. More expensive policies can cover you for 70 percent of your salary and more. Although losing 30 or 40 percent of your salary may sound like a big hardship, keep in mind that if you pay your premiums out-of-pocket, the disability benefits will not be subject to income tax. (That's because you paid your premiums out of money that has already been subject to tax.)

Disability policies may come with several different features. Some policies are non-cancelable and offer something called guaranteed renewability. This means that your policy cannot be canceled should your health deteriorate and that you are guaranteed the opportunity to renew your policy.

Another policy feature is called future insurability. Future insurability allows you to purchase more coverage even if your health declines. Although disability insurance is only sold to replace a portion of your income, future insurability allows you to increase your coverage, regardless of your health, in the event that your income increases. This feature is especially important for professionals who are pursuing additional training or degrees which, upon completion, will afford them a significant increase in salary.

A fourth policy feature to consider is a cost-of-living-adjustment (COLA). A COLA automatically increases the amount of the benefit by a specific percentage that is related to the cost of living. You are able to choose the percentage of the COLA when you purchase your policy. In the event you begin collecting a disability benefit, the COLA will increase your monthly benefit every year for the duration of your claim up to the maximum you elected. This means that if you purchase a 3 percent COLA, your benefit can increase up to 3 percent annually for as long as you collect benefits.

Another feature that is important is how the policy defines "disabled." For example, some policies will pay a benefit if you are unable to work in your particular profession or position. Even if you are able to work in some other capacity, they will still pay your benefit. This is called an "own-occupation" policy. For example, if you work as a carpenter and get hurt so badly you are unable to do physical labor, an own-occupation policy would pay benefits even if you could work in an office or clothing store. This is the most comprehensive form of disability insurance and is also the most expensive.

Some policies only pay a benefit if you are completely disabled and unable to work in any capacity. These types of policies, often referred to as Gainful Occupation Coverage, state that in order to receive benefits you must be unable to perform the duties of any job that you are deemed reasonably qualified to hold. This type of policy is typically the least expensive because it leaves a lot open to interpretation. In the event you file a claim, it may be difficult to get your claim approved.

If you do not have any long-term disability insurance, there are state and federal programs that may provide financial support in the event of a debilitating illness or injury. As we have already seen in Chapter 9, the Social Security Administration's disability program will pay long-term benefits if you have a disability that prevents you from working for at least a year. There are also state disability programs. These state-funded programs, however, are not usually meant to do more than cover you for more than a year. After that, you have to rely on Social Security.

You should be aware that just because you file a claim, it can be difficult to get approval. Indeed, 70 percent of all Social Security disability claims are denied. In addition, keep in mind that even if your claim is approved, the benefit is designed to only cover basic living expenses and is unlikely to be enough to allow you to maintain your current lifestyle.

Because there's a very real possibility that you will become disabled, experts advise electing coverage if your employer offers it. Your employer, after all, will pay at least part of your premium. If you have the option of purchasing additional disability coverage through your employer, it's a good idea to do so, since the out-of-pocket cost to you is likely to be quite modest. Should you need to purchase long-term disability coverage on your own, be sure to shop around for the lowest premiums. Also, if you purchase a policy from an agent, be sure to ask for something called list billing. This will allow you to sign up for coverage with several other people at the same time. List billing can save you up to 15 percent off the policy's premiums.

AUTO INSURANCE

Just about everyone who owns a car has to purchase some kind of auto insurance. In its most basic form, auto insurance protects you in the event that you are at fault in an automobile accident. Insurance can also protect you against losses that may occur due to theft or damage to your vehicle. When you purchase auto insurance you buy a policy that actually bundles together several different types of insurance. The cost of the policy is based on a number of factors, including your age, gender, number of years' driving experience, and the age and type of car you drive.

Some types of auto insurance aren't optional. For example, almost every state requires that drivers carry some form of liability insurance. This type of insurance covers damage you might do to another person and/or their vehicle in the event of an accident. The amount of liability insurance you are required to carry varies from state to state.

In addition to liability insurance, auto insurance companies offer other types of insurance that can be added to your policy. Collision insurance pays for damage to your vehicle in the event of an accident in which you're at fault or if someone damages your parked vehicle and drives away without leaving their name and contact information. Comprehensive insurance covers damage done to your car due to severe weather conditions (such as hail, wind, fire, or flood), theft, and vandalism.

You can also purchase medical coverage, which would pay medical expenses of a passenger who is injured in an auto accident. Insurance companies also sell Personal Injury Protection (PIP). PIP pays the medical expenses for the insured driver that are the result of a car accident; these benefits are paid regardless of who is at fault. Although PIP is not required by all states, it is required by some.

Finally, a few other types of insurance you can elect include uninsured motorist, underinsured motorist, and rental reimbursement coverage. Uninsured motorist coverage pays for damage to your car if you are involved in an accident with a person who does not have liability insurance. (Although driving without liability insurance is generally illegal, there are people who do so.) Similarly, underinsured motorist insurance protects you in the event you are in an accident with someone who does not carry enough liability insurance to cover the damage. Lastly, rental reimbursement coverage will pay for at least a portion of the cost of renting a car while your damaged vehicle is being repaired.

As is true of other financial decisions, it's important to do your research before choosing an auto insurance policy. A key thing to look at is the insurance company's reputation. Some companies are quicker in paying claims, for example. Friends and family can share their experiences with their insurance carriers, of course. There are also commercial rating services; Moody's Investor Services rates a number of insurance companies at their website www.moodys.com.

It's also worth noting that depending on what state you live in, you may be offered what is known as "no fault" insurance. This means that in the event of an accident, your insurance company pays for damage to your vehicle, regardless of who was at fault.

No matter what type of coverage your state requires you to carry, it's important to keep in mind that the minimum amount of insurance might not be adequate. If you're at fault in an accident and the damage you do is more than your coverage, you could be held responsible for the difference. When you buy your policy it is worth asking how much additional coverage would cost. Chances are good that for a relatively small additional premium, you can buy as much liability coverage as you're ever likely to need.

Another thing to keep in mind is that if you lease or finance your vehicle, the bank or finance company may require you to carry collision and comprehensive insurance. They will expect you to have enough coverage to protect their interest (what you owe for the vehicle) in the event that it is damaged or stolen. If you do not have sufficient coverage, the bank or finance company will hold you responsible for the remaining value of the car, even if it is no longer drivable or in your possession.

As with other types of insurance, it is always wise to shop around. Annual premiums can vary drastically from one company to another, so it is possible to get comparable coverage for money. Be aware, though, that some insurers quote premiums by the year, while others price their insurance in 6-month increments. Before you jump at what seems like an extremely cheap policy, make certain that you know what the policy's term is.

Another way to save is by increasing the deductible on your policy. Raising your deductible on collision or comprehensive insurance from $250 to $500 can save you 10 percent or more on your annual premium. Many insurance companies offer even higher deductibles. Just keep in mind that if you're carrying a $1,000 deductible and have an accident bad enough to disable your car, you'll have to find the money to get your car back into drivable condition.

Maintaining a good driving record is extremely important in keeping your auto insurance rates low. Speeding tickets, accidents, and drunk-driving convictions can dramatically raise your premiums or make it nearly impossible to get insurance at all. Tickets and accidents remain on your insurance record for three years, which is a long time to wait to return to lower rates. If you do find yourself getting a ticket for a moving violation, it's worth investigating whether your state's motor vehicle department has any driver-improvement programs. Some states will agree not to report your first moving violation to your insurance company if you complete an approved driver-improvement course.

Other ways to earn a low premium include reducing your commute. People who drive fewer miles each day get better rates than those who have long commutes. The logic behind this is that the less you drive, the less likely you are to have an accident. Also, living in a safe neighborhood, keeping your car in a garage, and installing anti-theft devices on your car will lower your premium. Insurance companies figure that these measures will protect your vehicle from being damaged or stolen.

Insurance companies also give price breaks for insuring more than one vehicle. Therefore, if you, your spouse, and a dependent child all have cars, you can save money by using the same auto insurer for all three cars.

Last, you can keep your premiums low by driving a vehicle that is considered cheaper to repair. Even though you can afford to buy a one-of-a-kind hand-built luxury car, you may be in for an unpleasant surprise at how expensive the insurance is. In addition, insurance companies charge higher rates for sports cars, since these tend to be expensive to repair.

HOMEOWNER'S/RENTERS INSURANCE

If you own a home, it is likely to be your most valuable possession. Therefore, it makes sense to protect it against damage or destruction. In the event of a natural disaster such as a fire or flood, or in the event that your home is robbed, a homeowner's policy would help offset the cost of rebuilding or replacing your possessions. In addition to protecting the structure itself, homeowners insurance protects items inside the home. It also protects you if someone sustains an injury while they are on your property. If you buy a house, your lender will likely require that you purchase homeowner's insurance prior to closing the sale.

Renters may also consider buying insurance. Although renters are not required to purchase insurance on the residence itself, it can be smart to buy a policy that protects the belongings inside the home, since the owner of the house or apartment will probably not be carrying more than insurance on the structure itself. Renter's insurance policies generally protect your possessions against fire, theft, and vandalism. Such a policy can also protect you against a liability lawsuit should someone be injured on the premises.

There are seven different types of homeowners insurance. Learn about each one so you can be sure you purchase the best one for your needs. The items listed as being covered under a particular policy are referred to as perils. The more perils you purchase coverage against, the higher your premium will be.

HO-1 covers the most common perils. These include fire, certain types of weather damage (including lightning), glass breakage, theft, property loss, explosions, riots, damage caused by a vehicle, or damage that may happen due to an airplane crash. HO-1 policies are limited in that they only provide coverage for items that are specifically outlined in the policy.

HO-2 policies cover all the perils covered by HO-1. In addition, they provide protection against a roof-collapse that might occur due to snow or ice; damage due to overheating or frozen water pipes; damage caused by malfunctioning central heating or air conditioning; collapse of a portion of your home; damage from falling objects; and damage to certain appliances as a result of an electrical surge. Also referred to as a "named perils" policy, HO-2 policies cover only the events that are spelled out in the policy.

HO-3 policies are the most commonly written policies. They cover the items listed under HO-1 and HO-2 policies and also the home's structure and contents. They also provide protection against your being sued by a visitor who gets injured while on your property. As with HO-1 and HO-2 policies, coverage must be specifically outlined within the policy.

HO-4 policies are ideal for renters. They cover items within the home as well as injuries from accidents in the home. These policies do not cover the structure itself.

HO-5 policies are similar to HO-3 policies but cover a wider spectrum of possible losses. HO-5 policies have certain eligibility requirements: your home must have been built after 1950, a smoke detector must be installed within the residence, you must have a hand-held fire extinguisher, and deadbolt locks must be installed on entrance doors. HO-5 provides the most extensive coverage, and for this reason it is also the most expensive.

HO-6 policies are also known as condominium coverage policies. They are designed specifically for the needs of condo owners. They include the portion of the building that is owned by the policyholder, items within the residence, and liability coverage.

HO-7 policies are similar to HO-1 policies in that they protect the home against the 11 most common perils. HO-7 policies also specifically cover older homes. They will cover replacement or repair for parts of the home that would have a higher replacement cost than their market value. This is a good policy if your home has certain architectural structures that would be costly to repair or if the home has historical significance.

Regardless of the perils covered, homeowner's insurance policies provide either actual cash value coverage or replacement coverage for items listed in the policy. Actual cash value policies cover your home and the items within it up to their depreciated value. For example, let's say you purchase a leather couch for $3,500 and 5 years later it is damaged due to some mishap that is covered under your policy. Because of depreciation, your insurance company may only reimburse you for a small fraction of the couch's original cost. The same goes for the home itself: the insurance company will start with the cost of your home and then calculate depreciation based on the age of the home. The amount you receive in such a case might not be anywhere near what you need to rebuild.

Replacement cost policies pay what it costs to replace the damaged or lost item. Replacement cost policies typically cost 10 percent more than cash value policies. But because they replace damaged, lost, or stolen items as though they were new, such policies can be worth the additional expense.

When shopping for homeowners insurance, it is always wise to ask the insurance company what is not covered. For example, some policies have limitations on the amount of coverage they provide for personal property lost to fire or theft. Jewelry, in particular, is typically only covered up to a certain limit (even under replacement value policies), and that figure may not correspond to the item's actual value. Recreational vehicles, such as jet-skis and motor boats, might not be covered by your homeowner's policy at all, even if you store them in your garage. In addition, many standard policies do not cover damage caused by a blocked sewer or other plumbing problem.

If your policy does not include all the coverage you want, you may be able to purchase something called a rider. Riders provide additional coverage for property that is not otherwise covered by an insurance policy. Riders are especially important if your possessions include valuable works of art or antiques. The cost of riders is usually not particularly high, considering the extra value they provide.

It's a good idea to make a video that shows the items in your home so as to have an accurate inventory of your belongings. This will ensure proper payment of your claim and help you remember what items you actually own. The video should be updated annually and should be stored outside of your home in a safe place (such as a safe deposit box).

One thing to be aware of is that damage caused by flooding or earthquakes is typically not covered by standard homeowner's insurance policies. Coverage against such events must be purchased separately. If you live in an area prone to floods or earthquakes, it is wise to obtain this coverage. Otherwise, you could be out tens of thousands of dollars should disaster strike.

Also keep in mind that just because you want a certain level of coverage does not mean that you will get it. The insurance industry as a whole keeps close track of claims through the Comprehensive Loss Underwriting Exchange (CLUE). CLUE tells insurance companies how many claims have been filed against a particular property and how much money has been paid out due to damages. Insurers may refuse to issue policies for houses that are prone to perils such as mold or water damage or may only insure the home in return for a much higher premium. For these reasons, when you purchase a home, be sure to request the current owner provide you with its CLUE report prior to finalizing the sale.

As with other types of insurance, opting for a higher deductible will save you money on your premiums. Purchasing your homeowner's insurance policy from the same company that insures your vehicle may get you a discount on both policies. Installing deadbolts, smoke detectors, burglar alarms, and other home safety items may also reduce your premium. If you live in an area that is prone to hurricanes, installing storm shutters will also allow for additional savings.

You might also be able to save a little money by paying your premium annually. Breaking your premium into quarterly or semi-annual payments may help your short-term cash flow, but it will come at an additional cost in the form of processing fees.

Buying insurance may be something you'd rather put off. After all, the range of choices can seem overwhelming. Also, the need may seem less-than-urgent. However, protecting the assets you've worked hard to build is well worth the time.

WORKSHEETS IN THIS CHAPTER:

- **Home Inventory Worksheet**: For insurance purposes, it is important to record the value, purchase date, and description of each item or piece of furniture in each room in your home.

- **Home Improvement Record Worksheet**: Home improvements can add substantially to the value of your house. Use this worksheet to keep a record of each project, cost, and timeline.

HOME INVENTORY WORKSHEET

ROOM:			ROOM:			ROOM:		
Item description	Date	Amount	Item description	Date	Amount	Item description	Date	Amount
Totals								

ROOM:			ROOM:			ROOM:		
Item description	Date	Amount	Item description	Date	Amount	Item description	Date	Amount
Totals								

Item description	Company	Phone number	Warranty info	Purchase date	Cost

THE IMPORTANCE
OF KEEPING RECORDS

As you have read through this book, you have likely noticed a recurring theme: keeping records is not only important, it is an absolute necessity. To keep track of your expenses, you'll need to keep records that show how your money is being spent. To protect yourself in the event of a tax audit, you will need to maintain records to back up the deductions you claim on your tax returns. There are some documents that are best kept in a safe deposit box and others that can be kept filed at home. The last chapter of this book will break down the importance of each document in question and help you decide how long to keep them and where best to store them.

DOCUMENTS BEST STORED IN A SAFE DEPOSIT BOX

Documents that are difficult or impossible to replace should be stored in a safe place away from the home. In the event of a fire or burglary, storing these documents away from your home makes it far less likely that they'll be destroyed or taken. These types of documents should be protected and include the following:

Birth Certificates
Although these can be replaced, doing so can be expensive and time consuming. The occasions when you need to produce an official birth certificate are relatively rare, so there's no real advantage to keeping it at home.

Death Certificates
Just as a state certificate is issued at the time of a person's birth, a similar certificate is issued upon a person's death. When a parent or other close relative you're caring for dies, you'll be issued a death certificate. If you're named as a beneficiary on any life insurance policies, you'll need to submit a copy of the insured person's death certificate in order to collect the benefit. For this reason, it's a good idea to keep this document secure.

Passports and Citizenship Papers
As with birth and death certificates, citizenship papers are documents that you will want kept safe. Replacing documents of this sort can be extremely time-consuming and expensive, so they are best kept in a safe deposit box.

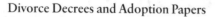

Divorce Decrees and Adoption Papers

In that divorce decrees and adoption papers are legal documents, they too should be stored in a safe place outside of the home. Although you can obtain copies through your attorney, ensuring the safety of the original documents can potentially save you a lot of stress, time, and expense. And if you need them quickly, you'll only have to wait until your bank is open, instead of waiting for your attorney to get you a copy.

Other Legal Documents

If the document in question is a legal one, the best rule of thumb is to store it in a safe deposit box. Titles to automobiles, property deeds, stock certificates, and bonds should always be stored outside of the home. In the event of a fire, flood, or burglary, these are documents you will not want to have to worry about replacing! If you are unsure whether a particular document should be stored in a safe deposit box, it is always best to err on the side of caution.

DOCUMENTS BEST STORED AT HOME

There are many documents that are important but do not need the extra protection of a safe deposit box. For example, your insurance paperwork need not be locked away at the bank where you cannot immediately get at it. Warranties on appliances and receipts for repairs to appliances and your car are best kept where you can immediately access them. All non-legal documents should be photocopied—in case the original gets misplaced. Car registration and insurance documents should be kept in your vehicle's glove compartment. If you are pulled over by the police, the officer will want to see those things right away (and if you're unable to produce one or both, you may be issued a ticket).

CONCLUSION

Many people feel uncomfortable dealing with financial matters, especially their own. Do you have negative feelings pertaining to money and try to avoid talking about it? Or, do you feel overwhelmed and inadequate when forced to pay bills or examine other financial matters? Such feelings diminish when you decide to take responsibility for your income and how you allocate it.

By reading this book, you have equipped yourself for achieving financial success. Now it is possible for you to enjoy the peace of mind that comes from taking an active role in planning for a secure and prosperous future. As philosopher Sir Francis Bacon famously stated, "Knowledge is power."

Once you determine your goals and know where you stand financially, you can calculate your net worth and put your budget into practice, using this book as your guide. Set aside time to complete your financial homework by scheduling certain days for financial tasks, such as researching mutual funds or reviewing your insurance coverage. Committing days on your calendar to take care of financial matters will ensure that your finances remain in the forefront of your mind and plans.

Take your next right step toward financial success by selecting a principle found in this book and carrying it out. That may be as straightforward as setting up a savings account or implementing a debt-payment plan. Success with your first step will lead to your second. With each step, you'll feel more confident to face your financial challenges. Remember to share your achievements with friends and family that support your financial accomplishments and independence. In this way, you control your money instead of your money controlling you.

Another key to financial success is realizing that only you can take control of your earnings and dictate how they should be distributed. Now that you've read this book, you know what it takes to master your finances. What remains is committing to a life that is financially responsible and proactive. Will concepts such as *avoid bad debt, pay yourself first,* and *invest wisely* have an effect on your day-to-day life? Only you can seize these ideas and implement them, and they in return will reward you with financial stability and success.

Most of all, grasp the concept that you must be actively involved in the ongoing management of your finances. Follow the recommendations in this book and cultivate a healthy financial plan that will sustain you and your family over time. By incorporating the guidelines you have learned here, your earnings and investments not only have the power to cover your needs now but also to enrich your life in later years. Your finances can be a source of pride and satisfaction instead of conflict and worry. Let *Personal Finance Made Easy* be the primary resource for achieving your financial goals.

THE *MADE EASY* SERIES

ABOUT THE AUTHOR OF THE *MADE EASY* SERIES

Alex A. Lluch is a seasoned entrepreneur with outstanding life achievements. Through hard work and dedication, he has become a self-made millionaire and one of the most successful authors and businessmen of our time. He is now using his expert knowledge to write the *Made Easy* series to help people succeed in finance, business, and real estate.

The following are a few of Alex's achievements:

- Author of over 3 million books sold in a wide range of categories: health, fitness, diet, home, finance, weddings, children, and babies
- President of WS Publishing Group, a successful publishing company
- President of WeddingSolutions.com, one of the world's most popular wedding planning websites
- President of UltimateGiftRegistry.com, an extensive website that allows users to register for gifts for all occasions
- President of a highly successful toy and candy company
- Designed complex communication systems for Fortune 500 companies
- Owns real estate in California, Colorado, Georgia and Montana
- B.S. in Electronics Engineering and an M.S. in Computer Science

Alex A. Lluch lives in San Diego, California with his wife of 16 years and their three wonderful children.

OTHER BOOKS IN THE *MADE EASY* SERIES

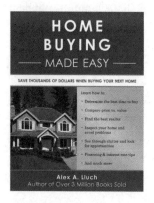

Learn how to:
- Determine the best time to buy
- Compare price vs. value
- Find the best realtor
- Inspect your home and avoid problems
- Financing and interest rate tips

Home Buying Made Easy is full of practical advice and hands-on worksheets to help homebuyers save thousands when making this important purchase! This informative guide includes everything homebuyers need to know when searching for and purchasing a home.

Learn how to:
- Stay organized and on-budget
- Minimize costly change orders
- Find the best contractors
- Save money on materials
- Minimize stress

Home Improvement Made Easy is full of comprehensive information and tips to get started on any size home-improvement project. Plus, it includes more than 100 easy-to-use worksheets to help the homeowner document each project.